Alpha to Ωmega

Activity Pack

Stage Three

Bevé Hornsby and Julie Pool

HEINEMANN
EDUCATIONAL

Heinmann Educational
a division of Heinmann Publishers (Oxford) Ltd
Halley Court, Jordan Hill, Oxford OX2 8EJ
OXFORD   LONDON   EDINBURGH
MADRID   ATHENS   BOLOGNA   PARIS
MELBOURNE   SYDNEY   AUCKLAND   SINGAPORE   TOKYO
IBADAN   NAIROBI   HARARE   GABORONE
PORTSMOUTH NH (USA)

A catalogue record for this book is available from
the British Library on request

ISBN 0 435 103873

Designed and Typeset by The Design Revolution, Brighton

Printed and bound by Athenaeum Press Ltd, Newcastle Upon Tyne

DEDICATION

To my husband, Tony Pool, whose support and guidance
have sustained us throughout this project.

ACKNOWLEDGEMENTS

Sam Fendrich – for his help and advice on the Maths Sheets.
My students, especially Jason Casanova, Jessica Gray,
Fatima Koura and Luke Williamson.

CONTENTS

CONTENTS

TEACHER'S NOTES

Answers are found on page 90 – 107

1 Syllable division and stress marking 1 This is the first of a series of sheets on syllable division and marking. The students should say the word out loud and divide it into syllables. They should then write the word as divided on the line next to the word and mark the stressed syllable and the vowel in that syllable (long '–' or short '˘'). The words on this sheet are all closed syllable words. Detailed instructions are on the sheet. This list is on pages 158–9 of *Alpha to Omega.*

2 Syllable division and stress marking 2 Same as for sheet 1. The words on this sheet contain an open vowel in the stressed syllable. Detailed instructions are on the sheet. This list is on pages 159–60 of *Alpha to Omega.*

3 Syllable division and stress marking 3 Same as for sheet 1. The words on this sheet contain only short vowel sounds, but there is only one consonant, and the syllable should be divided between the consonant and the following vowel. This list is on page 160 of *Alpha to Omega.*

4 Syllable division and stress marking 4 Same as for sheet 1. This sheet is a revision of the previous three sheets. This list is on page 161 of *Alpha to Omega.*

5 Syllable division and stress marking 5 Same as for sheet 1. This sheet consists of lazy 'e' words of more than one syllable. This list is on pages 161–2 of *Alpha to Omega.*

6 'r' trackings This sheet contains a series of three trackings: digraph '-r','rr', and a mixed tracking. In the digraph tracking the students are asked to set up a colour code. They should then track (from left to right) and highlight the words with the colour they have chosen in the colour code. When they have highlighted all of the words containing an '_r' digraph, they should track again and highlight the digraph in each word. Now they should divide the words into syllables and mark the stressed syllable. A colour code should also be established for the mixed tracking. This exercise is related to teaching on page 162 of *Alpha to Omega.*

7 Family trees The sheets presented here will help your students to understand how a family tree works.

A vocabulary list of relationship words has been included to help students understand the terminology. The first sheet for completion is a matching sheet based on the family tree of the royal family. It starts with the Queen's father and mother, King George VI and Lady Elizabeth Bowes-Lyon, and spreads to their great-grandchildren. The second is a blank tree for your students to fill in and make a family tree of their own. A sheet has been provided to give guidance, but they may also need to do some research for this sheet.

7b and c The royal family tree This matching sheet can be used by an individual student working on his/her own or by a group of students working together. It can also be used competitively (as a timed exercise or using different coloured pens) or co-operatively (discussing and working out the relationships). The object is for the students to answer the questions by drawing a line to the correct person.

7d and e Your family tree This sheet is for use by individual students, although it can be used as a group project. The sheet is self-explanatory, but it is very important that the students gather the necessary information before tackling the sheet.

8 'tion' tracking and definitions puzzle First the students are asked to find the real words in the tracking and highlight them. They should then divide them into syllables, marking the stressed syllable and the vowel in that syllable (long ' – ' or short '˘'). They should then do the Definitions Puzzle on the next page. All the real words in the tracking are listed here in alphabetical order for the students to check their answers. They are then asked to match each word to its definition by writing the word in the spaces next to the definition. When the puzzle is complete and correct, the column in bold will read: **Be proud of this noble effort! It is a complete success!** This exercise is related to teaching on pages 163–4 of *Alpha to Omega.*

9 'tion' transformations matching The students are asked to match the list of verbs to the jumbled list of nouns and to write the matching noun on the line provided. The students should then say the noun aloud and mark the stressed syllable and the vowel in that syllable (long or short). When they have completed the list, they should choose ten of the nouns and write a sentence using each in their exercise books. This exercise is similar to the exercise on page 165 in *Alpha to Omega*.

TEACHER'S NOTES

10 Dark/l/triple tracking and fill 'em ups. This exercise contains a series of three trackings: 'le' at the end of the word, '_l' words and a mixed tracking. Fill 'em ups is a sheet of sentences using most of the real words in the tracking which the students should try to complete. This exercise is related to teaching on pages 166–7 of **Alpha to Omega**.

11 Proofreading This exercise asks the students to read the paragraph and to use conjunctions to join the sentences together where it seems reasonable. Some conjunctions have been suggested but others may be used and words can be changed where necessary. Be sure that the students have changed the punctuation in the paragraph. When proofreading is completed, the students should copy the paragraph into their exercise books. This exercise is related to the exercise on page 174 of **Alpha to Omega**.

12 Misleading information All the sentences in this exercise need to be corrected by the students. They should write the corrected sentences on the lines provided. This is an extended version of the exercise on page 175 of **Alpha to Omega**.

13 Multiple choice suffixing This exercise asks the students to select and write in the correct spelling of the 'root word' + a suffix. Before attempting this exercise they should understand the rule and word list of Suffixing II on page 176 of **Alpha to Omega**.

14 Advanced active–passive roundabouts The students are asked to change the active sentences to passive ones and the passive sentences to active ones. The new sentences should be written on the lines provided. There are five sentences in each group. This exercise is a revised version of the exercise on page 178 in **Alpha to Omega**; it is quite difficult and should only be given to advanced students.

15 Passive transformations The students are shown step by step how to change an active sentence to a negative passive sentence with a qualifying phrase. They are then asked to change it into a question and answer it. A sheet is provided for this work on the following page. This exercise is similar to the exercise on pages 179–80 in **Alpha to Omega**.

16 Reported speech jumbled roundabouts This sheet gives a brief demonstration of how dialogue questions are turned into reported speech. This is

followed by a series of three exercises. In the first exercise the students are presented with two sentences – one is a dialogue question to be turned into reported speech, the other is a sentence in reported speech to be turned into a dialogue question. (NB The answer to this can use 'must' or 'have to'.) In the second exercise there are four dialogue questions which have been jumbled. These should be sorted so they can be combined to make two sentences in reported speech. In the third exercise this procedure is reversed: there are two sentences in reported speech which can make four dialogue questions. This is a revised version of the exercise on page 181 in **Alpha to Omega**.

17 Tricky tracking–'our' and 'gh' This sheet consists of two trackings: one for the different sounds of 'our', and the other for 'gh' saying /f/ and 'gh' as silent.

For the 'our' tracking your students will need three coloured pens or highlighters. First they are asked to track for real and nonsense words, crossing out the nonsense words. Then they are asked to create a colour code for the three sounds of 'our' and to mark the words according to their colour code. This exercise should follow the teaching on pages 181–2 in **Alpha to Omega**.

The 'gh' tracking requires two coloured pens or highlighters. First ask your students to track for the 'gh' saying /f/ words and to highlight them. Then the students should go back to the beginning of the tracking and highlight the silent 'gh' words. They will know they are correct if the /f/ words form an 'F' in the middle of the tracking. This exercise should follow the teaching on pages 188–9 in **Alpha to Omega**.

18 'ch' tracking and definitions puzzle First the students are asked to select three different coloured pens or highlighters and to use them, one at a time to track for the three sounds of 'ch' – /ch/, /k/, /sh/. When they have done the tracking three times, they should do the Definitions Puzzle. This is self-marking and is a check for the tracking. When the puzzle is complete, the sentence reading down the puzzle in bold reads: **Each step in learning leads to understanding. Well done!** In the puzzle the 'ch' sound is /k/ in words 1–19, /sh/ in words 20–30 and /ch/ in words 31–46. This exercise relates to teaching on pages 183–4 in **Alpha to Omega**.

TEACHER'S NOTES

19 /k/ multiple choice spellings The students should read each sentence and write the correct spelling for each of the missing words in the spaces provided. They should then write each completed sentence on the line(s) provided. This exercise relates to teaching on pages 183–6 of *Alpha to Omega*.

20 /f/ fill 'em ups The students are asked to read the paragraph and fill in the missing 'f', 'gh' or 'ph'. They should then write in the completed words in the lists below. This exercise relates to teaching on pages 187–9 of *Alpha to Omega*.

21 Conditional and cause and effect matching This exercise asks the students to match the beginning of each sentence with the correct ending. They should write the completed sentences in their exercise books. This is a revised version of the exercise on pages 190–1 in *Alpha to Omega*.

22 /a/ multiple choice spellings The students are asked to choose the correct spelling of the missing word and to write the correct spelling in the space provided. They should then write the completed sentence on the line(s) provided. This exercise relates to teaching on page 193 in *Alpha to Omega*.

23 Wornout words The students are asked to read each paragraph which contains one over-exposed word. The word is highlighted in bold. They are then asked to re-write each paragraph on the lines provided replacing (or not using) the highlighted word. This is a revised and extended version of the exercise on page 189 of *Alpha to Omega*.

24 'ti' and 'ci' marathon This is a series of three exercises using words which include 'ti' and 'ci' saying /sh/.

Identify the profession– 'cian' In this first exercise the students are given a profession and asked to define it, including the root word in their definition.

Mixed matching The second exercise includes two lists of words: the 'ti'/'ci' words and related words. The students are asked to write the related words to the 'ti'/'ci' words in the column. They may need to use a dictionary to understand fully the meanings of some of these words. At the end of this exercise they are asked to write a sentence in their exercise books for each 'ti'/'ci' word using the related word as well.

Multiple choice endings In the third exercise the students are asked to choose the correct spelling of the 'ti'/'ci' word and to write it in the space provided. They should then write the completed sentence on the line below.

These exercises relate to teaching on pages 194–5 in *Alpha to Omega*.

25a Tricky tracking– 'sion' and 'ssion' The students are asked to find the correctly spelled words in these two trackings and to highlight them. These words are very good for syllable division as well as vowel and stress marking. This can be done after the original tracking exercise. This exercise relates to teaching on pages 195–7 in *Alpha to Omega*.

25b Verb–noun puzzle The students are presented with a list of verbs and are asked to write in the appropriate noun. All the words in this puzzle are included in the two previous trackings. If they have answered the puzzle correctly, the column in bold will read down as follows: **Excellent! Success is super.** The first twelve words in the puzzle are 'sion' words; the rest are 'ssion' words. When they have finished the puzzle, they should go back to the trackings and check that they have highlighted the correct words. The students should then write sentences using the nouns and the verbs.

26 /shən/ proofreading This exercise is a consolidation and revision exercise for all the spellings of /sh n/ which have now been taught: 'tion', 'cian', 'sion', 'ssion'. The students are asked to read the paragraph and correct the mis-spellings. They are then asked if they found 46 mistakes. After completing this exercise, they should copy the corrected paragraph into their exercise books.

27 Tricky tracking– 'i' says /i/ and /y/ together This tracking consists of real words only. Some contain 'i' saying the combined sound of /i/ and /y/; others have 'i' saying /˘/, /¯/, or /˜/. The students are asked to find the words containing the combined sound: /i/ and /y/. These words should be highlighted. They should then go on to the next exercise which is on the same page. This exercise relates to teaching on pages 197–8 in *Alpha to Omega*.

Definitions puzzle This exercise is self-marking and makes the tracking self-marking. The students are asked to write in the words from the tracking which are defined in the puzzle. When the puzzle is correct, the sentence in bold will read as follows: **You are correct and clever!** These exercises relate to teaching on pages 197–8 in *Alpha to Omega*.

28 Multiple choice endings–'ture', 'ure' and 'gue' This exercise asks the students to select the correctly spelled word. All the endings include a 'u': 'ture' saying /cher/, 'ure' saying /er/ or 'gue' where the 'ue' is silent. The students are asked to write the correctly spelled word on the line next to the choice, and then to write the completed sentence on the line(s) provided. This exercise relates to work on pages 198–9 in *Alpha to Omega*.

29 More wornout words Same as for sheet 23 – Wornout words.

30 'er', 'or' and 'ar' definitions puzzle The words defined in this puzzle are listed at the top of the sheet. The students should match the words to the definitions. If the puzzle is filled in correctly, the sentence down the column in bold will read: **Achievement creates satisfaction.** The puzzle is divided into three sections: the first eleven words are 'er' words, the next ten words are 'or' words, and the last nine words are 'ar' words. This exercise relates to teaching on pages 199–200 in *Alpha to Omega*.

31 'ery', 'ary', 'ory' fill 'em ups This is a word completion exercise; all the words are from the list at the top of the page. The endings of the 'ery', 'ary', 'ory' words have been provided in the sentences. It is the students' job to complete the words. This exercise relates to teaching on pages 201–2 in *Alpha to Omega*.

32 Homophones crossword All of the words included in this puzzle are listed on the page below the grid. The clues are listed on the following pages. The students must know the meaning(s) of each word to complete the puzzle successfully. This exercise is related to teaching on pages 203–4 of *Alpha to Omega*.

33 Confusable words This sheet presents two pairs of words which are often confused because they look and sound very similar. The words are **affect** and **effect** and **bought** and **brought.** The most common use of these words is explained and is followed by an exercise using these words for the students to complete. For **affect** and **effect** the students could

look these words up in their dictionaries and use them in their other meanings. For **bought** and **brought** they should write several sentences of their own using both words.

34 Confusable words fill 'em ups This is a continuation of the preceding exercise except that the students should look up the words to find out the differences in meaning. They should then complete the sentences. Some of the words have more than one meaning; in these cases the students should write their own sentences to show the distinctions.

35 Silent letters tracking and Crossword All the words in this tracking have at least one silent letter. The students are asked to track from left to right, highlighting the silent letter(s). They should read the words aloud. After they have completed this, they should do the crossword below which contains all the words in the tracking. This exercise relates to teaching on pages 205–6 in *Alpha to Omega*.

36 Silent letter clues This sheet shows the students how some words which contain a silent letter say the silent letter when a suffix is added to the 'root' word. After each pair of words is presented, the students are asked to write their own sentences to create their own mnemonics. The last word presented is 'sign' and has a page of its own. Twenty words derived from 'sign' are presented for students to sort out into the ones containing a silent 'g' and the ones saying /g/. They should then write as many sentences as possible containing at least one word from each list.

37 Mapwork This is a series of exercises which is divided into three sections: Map of the European Community, Map of the British Isles and Map of the world.

Map of the European Community The first challenge is for the students to match the list of countries with the list of capitals. The capital letter (located on the left of the name of each capital city) should be written next to the name of its country on the lines in the middle of the page. When completed correctly, the column down the middle of the page will read: FUDGING BLIPS which can be re-arranged to read GLIB PIGS FUND. These are mnemonics made by using the first letter of each country's name to help the students remember which countries are in the European Community.

TEACHER'S NOTES

The students are then asked to match the numbers on the map of Europe to the numbers on the first sheet and to write in the names of the countries and capitals which belong to the European Community. They should colour the countries in the European Community in blue and the other countries in Europe in red. (NB The authors have felt it necessary to limit this exercise to the European Community as the shape of Europe is very changeable at the time of writing.)

Map of the British Isles The students are asked to answer a series of questions and to write in the names of the countries and capitals on the map. They should colour in the countries.

Map of the world The students are asked a series of questions, most of which can be answered by using the map. It would be advisable to have a world atlas available to your students to complete these exercises.

These exercises are related to teaching on pages 207–8 of *Alpha to Omega.* (A, B and C Matching Game of Countries and Capitals is available through The Hornsby Centre, 71 Wandsworth Common Westside, London SW18 2ED.)

38 Prefix and suffix matching This exercise is divided into two sections: the first is on prefixes, the second on suffixes. The students are asked to match the prefix (suffix) to its meaning in the opposite column by drawing a line to join them. This exercise relates to teaching on pages 211–12 in *Alpha to Omega.*

39 Classical tracking –prefixes and suffixes, and Definitions puzzle The first exercise asks students to track for words using classical prefixes and suffixes; the second is a definitions puzzle which uses the words in the tracking. All of the words in the tracking are to be matched with their definitions in the puzzle. The first thirty in the puzzle have classical prefixes, while the last eight have classical suffixes. The column in bold reading down says: **You are so clever and an excellent student too!** making this exercise (and the tracking) self-marking. This exercise relates to teaching on pages 212–3 in *Alpha to Omega.*

40a and b Exam words This sheet – the first in a series of four word sheets – presents thirty-six words which are frequently found in GCSE and other exams.

Most of the words are not specific to any one subject or exam, but are in general use. Where the word is relevant to one particular subject, this has been noted in brackets. Most of the words on this sheet are verbs, instructing students how to answer the question(s); if the word is or can be another part of speech, this has been noted. The students should learn the words and how to spell them using the look, cover, write, check method and their meanings. It would be helpful to give students sample exam questions using these terms; they could thereby see their use, learn their meaning and gain experience of using the terms. This exercise is followed by a definitions puzzle, as is each of the following subject-specific word sheets.

40c Exam words definitions puzzle contains all of the words presented on the previous sheet; they are listed at the top of the page to be tracked, if desired, and crossed off as they are placed in the puzzle. When the puzzle is correctly completed, the column in bold should read: **Understanding is your path to exam success.**

41a Maths words This sheet presents twenty-eight words which are frequently found in the Maths GCSE. Ask students to do the same as for Exam words.

41b Maths definitions puzzle Same as for Exam words definitions puzzle. The column in bold should read: **A maths success! Congratulations.**

42a and b Science words Thirty-five words relating to Science GCSE are presented in this sheet. Ask students to do the same as for Exam words.

42c Science definitions puzzle. Same as for Exam words definitions puzzle. The column in bold should read: **A top stepping stone to success in science.**

43 Science prefix and suffix matching This sheet contains two sections: one on prefixes and one on suffixes. The prefixes and suffixes should be introduced and explained to the students in relation to the science work. At the end of each section there is a matching exercise for the students to complete.

44 Science confusables This sheet consists of words which are easily confused in the Science GCSE syllabus. The students should learn the spellings, meanings and uses of the words and should see how

x

TEACHER'S NOTES

they are used within the science syllabus. Athough
sentences have been provided, it will be necessary to
give the students practice in using these words in
practical situations.

45 **Checklist for** *Alpha to Omega* **– Stage Three.**
This checklist, devised by Patience Thomson, is
designed to help the teacher keep a record of the
concepts learned as each child progresses through
Alpha to Omega. Please note that this sheet refers
only to the ***Alpha to Omega*** Handbook, not to the
Activity Pack; the following sections are found only in
the Handbook: Writing Plays, Proverbs, Girls' Names,
Boys' Names and Surnames.

Syllable Division and Stress Marking–1

1

Divide each of the words below into two syllables. Close the first syllable with a consonant because the vowel is **short**. Write the divided word on the lines provided. Then mark the **stressed** syllable with '′' and put the short vowel sign '˘' over **the vowel in the stressed syllable.** The first three have been done for you.

dentist	dĕń/tist______	assist	______________	clammy	______________
magnet	măǵ/net _____	gallon	______________	scandal	______________
intend	in/tĕńd______	lettuce	______________	suggest	______________
passage	______________	ransom	______________	success	______________
flannel	______________	horrid	______________	collect	______________
funny	______________	puppy	______________	village	______________
tennis	______________	muggy	______________	fellow	______________
pistol	______________	dummy	______________	yellow	______________
splendid	______________	Mummy	______________	pillow	______________
trumpet	______________	ugly	______________	shallow	______________
velvet	______________	hungry	______________	lumber	______________
disgust	______________	tunnel	______________	army	______________
window	______________	puppet	______________	sister	______________
willow	______________	insult	______________	Mister	______________
follow	______________	sultry	______________	master	______________
hollow	______________	mutton	______________	lantern	______________
infant	______________	button	______________	rabbit	______________
pregnant	______________	suspect	______________	butter	______________
seldom	______________	muslin	______________	letter	______________
perhaps	______________	hundred	______________	stopper	______________

In these words the vowel in the **stressed** syllable is **long** and so it will be in an **open** syllable (ending in a vowel).

Divide each of the words below into syllables; write the divided word on the line provided, mark the stress, and the vowel in the stressed syllable with the **long** vowel sign '‾'. The first three have been done for you.

acorn	á̄/corn ____	slogan	_____	duty	_____
humid	hū́/mid ____	vital	_____	climax	_____
torpedo	tor/pé̄/do __	nylon	_____	crazy	_____
label	_____	cupid	_____	gravy	_____
libel	_____	tulip	_____	Navy	_____
even	_____	evil	_____	legal	_____
crocus	_____	halo	_____	pony	_____
final	_____	robot	_____	local	_____
decent	_____	cider	_____	tiger	_____
recent	_____	spider	_____	vacant	_____
basin	_____	volcano	_____	baby	_____
Roman	_____	poem	_____	lady	_____
pupil	_____	lazy	_____	pilot	_____
idol	_____	agent	_____	diet	_____
hero	_____	regent	_____	paper	_____
holy	_____	rival	_____	later	_____
Peter	_____	Egypt	_____	lethal	_____
open	_____	Simon	_____	April	_____

Divide these words into syllables. Only one consonant follows the short vowel in these words, so we need to keep that consonant with the vowel. Divide the syllable after the consonant and before the vowel as shown in the examples below. Don't forget to mark the stress and the vowels (long or short). The first three have been done for you.

atom	ăt/om _____	radish	_____	manage	_____
Briton	Brĭt/on_____	punish	_____	widow	_____
modern	mŏd/ern ___	finish	_____	shadow	_____
lyric	_____	civic	_____	prison	_____
rigid	_____	civil	_____	seven	_____
linen	_____	digit	_____	study	_____
menu	_____	suburb	_____	spirit	_____
robin	_____	vomit	_____	parallel	_____
tenor	_____	frolic	_____	travel	_____
never	_____	profit	_____	Paris	_____
ever	_____	proper	_____	method	_____
Helen	_____	rapid	_____	Latin	_____
lily	_____	limit	_____	livid	_____
cabin	_____	body	_____	lemon	_____
credit	_____	promise	_____	present	_____
visit	_____	determine	_____	triple	_____
habit	_____	develop	_____	treble	_____
shrivel	_____	devil	_____	product	_____
magic	_____	damage	_____	level	_____
peril	_____	liver	_____	quiver	_____

Divide the words below into syllables and mark the stress. They are words with mixed patterns, so be careful. Write the divided words and mark the stress on the lines provided.

modern	_____	husband	_____	public	_____
conduct	_____	collect	_____	provide	_____
confide	_____	industry	_____	publish	_____
confidence	_____	interest	_____	pupil	_____
congress	_____	December	_____	protest	_____
connect	_____	introduce	_____	progress	_____
consist	_____	diamond	_____	problem	_____
contract	_____	letter	_____	produce	_____
district	_____	latter	_____	propose	_____
direct	_____	later	_____	protect	_____
select	_____	motor	_____	police	_____
divide	_____	moment	_____	polite	_____
except	_____	native	_____	prevent	_____
distant	_____	notice	_____	matter	_____
duty	_____	number	_____	comply	_____
dial	_____	offer	_____	sudden	_____
effort	_____	September	_____	suffer	_____
effect	_____	over	_____	supper	_____
establish	_____	remember	_____	subject	_____

Lazy 'e' words

All of these words are lazy 'e' words of more than one syllable. Divide them into syllables and mark the vowel (long or short) in the stressed syllable.

a_e

invade _____

lemonade _____

relate _____

mistake _____

translate _____

compare _____

welfare _____

dictate _____

brigade _____

e_e

compete _____

complete _____

athlete _____

extreme _____

concrete _____

supreme _____

delete _____

revere _____

interfere _____

i_e

alive _____

alike _____

inside _____

divide _____

polite _____

revive _____

advise _____

despite _____

o_e

alcove _____

propose _____

remote _____

explode _____

revoke _____

dispose _____

impose _____

invoke _____

u_e

amuse _____

assume _____

confuse _____

capsule _____

salute _____

contribute _____

gratitude _____

produce _____

introduce _____

reduce _____

'r' TRACKINGS

Digraph tracking – ar/er/ir/ur

Find the words with the vowel–consonant digraph '_r' and highlight the words with one colour. Then go back to the beginning and highlight the vowel–consonant digraph '_r' in those words, with another colour. Always work from left to right, starting at the top and working towards the bottom. Now divide the highlighted words into syllables and mark the vowels.

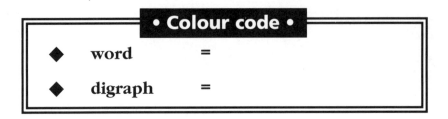

circlemejinhardtupbigenmurderwidglrFebruaryjuckenstartwehenburst
figotshortkrundleshuneccertainpraddlepurchasefodgrumbirthvunreds
stormbaddlehidremservicepumbritchurchklintinghonvrethirstyekkies
Septemberjadlupgofrupcornerprometurgentcraotrinfarmertrimepserve

'rr' tracking

Find the words with 'rr'. Highlight each word as you find it; then divide it into syllables, marking the stress.

barrowmurrpebtremlesquirrelvirtensorrydoputermarryankerrormikup
hickmupmirrortadgrentomorrowgruplefunterhurrybafnicharrivejibrr
correctpilkumdimrecurrentmeylrejefvumarrangestimplehorrorgumpes
berrymirpedlorrykefuprcurryplerunkquarrelstreplerfrumkterrormik

Mixed tracking

Now find the words with '_r' or 'rr'. First track for the words with an 'r' digraph '_r' and highlight them with one colour; then track for the 'rr' words and highlight each word containing 'rr' with another colour. Now divide the words into syllables, marking the stress.

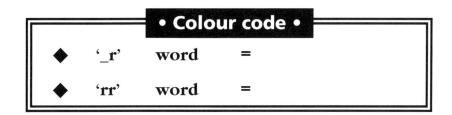

worrytenderfurtherflurrybrothercorrectsuburbOctobermerryworry
sharpMarchparrotsportmothernarrowerregardmirrorJanuarysorrow
sortsurrenderreturntargetstircarrysurprisefatherborrowDecember
lumberarrowNovemberhorridThursdayterrorSaturdaycarpet

FAMILY TREES

A family tree is like a great oak tree – it spreads with each generation. The tree is quite narrow at the top where the old branches are dying off, but it spreads at the bottom where new branches are growing.

At the top of a family tree you often find great-grandparents or other ancestors you have never known, and at the bottom you will find yourself or your children.

Two sheets presented here will help you understand how a family tree works. The first is the family tree of the Royal Family. The royal family tree starts with the Queen's father and mother, King George VI and his wife, Lady Elizabeth Bowes-Lyon (The Queen Mother), and spreads to their great-grandchildren. The second is a blank tree for you to fill in and make your own family tree. You may need to do some research for this. Ask your relations if they can help you.

Below is a list of words often used to describe relationships in a family. You may find it useful.

Vocabulary

spouse: a person's partner in marriage

mother-in-law: a partner's mother

father-in-law: a partner's father

son-in-law: a daughter's husband

daughter-in-law: a son's wife

sister-in-law: a partner's sister or a partner's brother's wife

brother-in-law: a partner's brother or a partner's sister's husband

niece: a brother's or sister's daughter

nephew: a brother's or sister's son

grandmother: a parent's mother

grandfather: a parent's father

aunt: a parent's sister

uncle: a parent's brother

first cousin: the child of an aunt or uncle

great-grandmother: a parent's grandmother

great-grandfather: a parent's grandfather

great-grandchild: the child of a grandchild

great-aunt: the sister of a grandparent

great-uncle: the brother of a grandparent

Who am I? matching

1 Who is Prince Philip's mother-in-law?

The Queen Mother

2 Who is Prince Edward's father?

Queen Elizabeth II

3 Who is Prince Charles's mother?

Prince Philip,
Duke of Edinburgh

4 Who is Princess Eugenie's father?

Princess Margaret

5 Who is Princess Anne's eldest nephew?

Antony Armstrong-Jones,
Earl of Snowdon

6 Who is Zara Phillips' youngest uncle?

Charles, Prince of Wales

7 Who is Princess Beatrice's oldest first cousin?

Diana, Princess of Wales

8 Who is the Queen's eldest son?

Anne, Princess Royal

9 Who is the Duke of York's youngest first-cousin?

Captain Mark Phillips

10 Who is Princess Eugenie's great aunt?

Prince Andrew, Duke of York

11 Who is Princess Margaret's niece?

Sarah, Duchess of York

12 Who is the Queen's youngest grandchild?

Prince Edward

13 Who is the Queen's nephew?

Viscount Linley

14 Who is the Queen Mother's second grandson?

Lady Sarah Armstrong-Jones

15 Who is the Queen's third grandson?

Prince William

16 Who is Princess Anne's eldest niece?

Prince Henry (Harry)

17 Who is Prince William's grandfather?

Peter Phillips

18 Who is the Queen's eldest granddaughter?

Zara Phillips

19 Who is Princess Beatrice's great-grandmother?

Princess Beatrice

20 Who is Viscount Linley's youngest first cousin?

Princess Eugenie

THE ROYAL FAMILY TREE

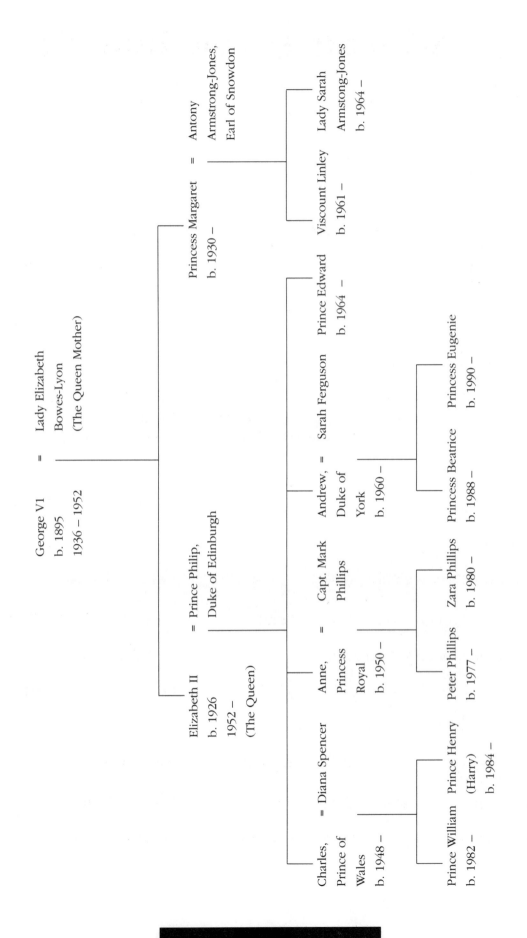

George V1
b. 1895
1936 – 1952

= Lady Elizabeth
Bowes-Lyon
(The Queen Mother)

Elizabeth II
b. 1926
1952 –
(The Queen)

= Prince Philip,
Duke of Edinburgh

Princess Margaret
b. 1930 –

= Antony
Armstrong-Jones,
Earl of Snowdon

Charles,
Prince of
Wales
b. 1948 –

= Diana Spencer

Anne,
Princess
Royal
b. 1950 –

= Capt. Mark
Phillips

Andrew, =
Duke of
York
b. 1960 –

Sarah Ferguson

Prince Edward
b. 1964 –

Viscount Linley
b. 1961 –

Lady Sarah
Armstong-Jones
b. 1964 –

Prince William
b. 1982 –

Prince Henry
(Harry)
b. 1984 –

Peter Phillips
b. 1977 –

Zara Phillips
b. 1980 –

Princess Beatrice
b. 1988 –

Princess Eugenie
b. 1990 –

YOUR FAMILY TREE

To complete your family tree of four generations, you will first have to decide which side of the family you want to use to make your tree: your mother's side or your father's side. You will need information from them about their parents and brothers and sisters to complete the tree. The tree on the next page is a guide to help you. Remember you will need as many lines for each generation as there are children.

1 On the top line of your tree write the name of your grandparents (either your mother's parents or your father's parents). It is often written like this: Mary Smith = Tom Jones. The = sign means 'married to'. Or you can write 'm.' for married.

2 On the next line you will see that there is more than one space for names. These spaces are for you to write in the name of your parent and the name of his/her spouse (your other parent) and the names of any brothers or sisters which this parent has (your aunts and uncles). You should also write in the names of the brothers' and sisters' spouses.

3 The next line is for you and your generation. Underneath your parents you write your name and the names of your brothers and sisters on the lines attached to your parents. If you or your brothers or sisters are married, write = and the spouse's name next to it. You can also write in the names of the children of your aunts and uncles (your first cousins).

4 The last line is for your children, and your brothers' and sisters' children, if there are any.

5 Now make a family tree for the other side of your family – your father's side or your mother's side, whichever you didn't do the first time.

YOUR FAMILY TREE

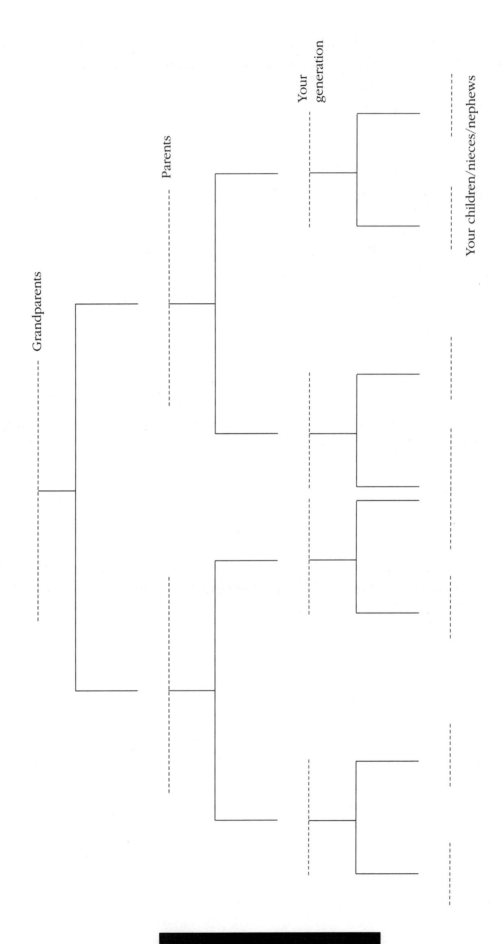

Grandparents

Parents

Your generation

Your children/nieces/nephews

'tion' TRACKING

Can you find the real words in this tracking? Circle or highlight the real word. Underline the 'tion' ending in a different colour. Now divide each real word into syllables, marking the stressed syllable and the vowel in that syllable (long or short).

interreption mention quorstion addition ambition doceration
mistion question contreption auction direction formution
perspiration protuction correction kindversetion resiption
protaction cerculetion exhibition infermation relation oction
action exemination reciption motion prepisition decoration
enterpertetion completion sujestion fruitition selection election
competition decition repatition prescription quistion hesitation
illution politition sensation intendtion inspiction position
preperation information ejercation section frection exhobation
function miniation examination conversation repertation station
eliction reception prepersition cansoderation recommendation
eksemination interpretation foundation ginerution compersition
subscription spation nation kerection muntion preparation trition
digestion suggestion protection serklation destruction
emagernation perfection condetion imformation elation jumption
subtraction estention attention postion education perscription
consideration

Did you find forty-four words? All the words hidden in the tracking are listed on the next page. Do you know what all the words mean? Match the words to the definitions by writing the correct word in the box next to the definition.

8b 'tion' DEFINITIONS PUZZLE

action	1	Club dues.
addition	2	Learning at school.
ambition		
attention	3	Place where something is.
auction	4	Something added to attract.
competition	5	Safety; keeping safe.
completion	6	Ruin, end, usually violent.
consideration	7	A plus sum.
conversation		
correction	8	Movement.
decoration	9	Knowledge; news.
destruction	10	North is a ___.
digestion	11	A thoughtful pause.
direction	12	Desire for success, goal.
education	13	A feeling through the senses
elation		
election	14	A country.
examination	15	Great delight; happiness.
exhibition	16	A take away sum.
foundation	17	Someone in your family.
function	18	A large informal gathering.
hesitation		
information	19	Something you ask.
interpretation	20	Base on which to build.
mention	21	Complete and flawless.
motion	22	To say something in passing.
nation	23	Talking; discussion.
perfection	24	A part or bit of something.
perspiration		
position	25	You take this to the chemist.
preparation	26	This is where a train stops.
prescription		
protection	27	A test at the end of a course.
question	28	Thoughtfulness.
reception		
recommendation	29	An act; what happens.
relation		
section	30	A good suggestion.
selection	31	A game or challenge.
sensation	32	Finishing or ending work.
station	33	Sweat; moisture from the skin.
subscription	34	Time to vote or choose a person.
subtraction	35	Give your work all of this.
suggestion	36	An explanation of a meaning.
	37	A public show or display.
	38	Choice.
	39	A sale by bidding.
	40	Purpose; use of something.
	41	Putting right an error.
	42	Making something ready.
	43	A hint; a clue.
	44	Bodily breakdown of food.

Read what it says about you in the highlighted boxes.

Match the verbs below to the jumbled nouns opposite; write the noun on the line next to the verb it matches. Say the noun and mark the stressed syllable(s). Then mark the vowel in the stressed syllable(s) to indicate whether it is long or short.

verbs		nouns
to perfect	_____	destruction
to compete	_____	addition
to destroy	_____	reception
to direct	_____	exclamation
to consider	_____	separation
to separate	_____	devotion
to propose	_____	prescription
to form	_____	preparation
to prescribe	_____	population
to receive	_____	creation
to inspect	_____	generation
to prepare	_____	consideration
to elect	_____	conversation
to inform	_____	formation
to devote	_____	examination
to compose	_____	perfection
to generate	_____	election
to exclaim	_____	direction
to examine	_____	digestion
to populate	_____	proposition
to converse	_____	composition
to add	_____	inspection
to digest	_____	information
to create	_____	competition

Choose ten of these nouns and write a sentence using each in your exercise book.

Many words end in a dark/l/ sound, but they can be spelt in different ways.

'le' tracking

Find the real words in this tracking and circle (or highlight) them.
Underline (or use another colour to highlight) the '_le' ending.

bugle	twindle	possible	jamble	eagle	cupable	tripple	rifle
table	sirkle	angle	idle	bendle	wrinkle	truble	cradle	whistle
rinkle	cattle	perple	torrable	buddle	wiggle	simple	stuble
settle	jengle	spectacle	dimble	sensible	mabble	sparkle
circle	hurible	apple	terble	riffle	capable	sensble	uncle
mercle	botle	jugle	handle	kable	themble	battle	jigle

Exceptions tracking

Find the real words and use your pencils (or highlighters) to show the word and the ending.

circal	peepal	pencil	possibul	tunnel	perpel	metal
birdal	label	uncel	cathedral	jewel	sampal	hospital
cabil	original	sensibul	usual	vitel	special	obstacal	gradual

Mixed tracking

Now see if you can find the real words in this mixture of /l/ words. Use your pencils (or highlighters) to mark the words and the endings.

castle	miserbel	camel	medal	drizzle	general	cuddle
channel	traval	bottle	animal	bubble	trifel	sensible
appel	twiddle	sampal	maple	drissal	pupil	fatal	travel

Now complete the exercise on the next page.

I hope you have found all the real words because many of them are used in the sentences below. Now fill in the blanks. (Hint: the ending for each word is written for you as a clue but be careful because sometimes it is changed slightly from the version on sheet 10a. The number of dashes before the ending is a clue to how many letters are in the word.)

1 A _ _ _ el is an _ _ _ _ al which lives in the desert.

2 After the _ _ _ le sounded, the _ _ _ _ le began; the soldiers fought bravely with their _ _ _ les.

3 The _ _ _ _ le is full of water which shimmers and _ _ _ _ _ les.

4 The _ _ _ ils in this class are very bright and _ _ _ _ _ le of producing very good work; they will show you how _ _ _ _ le it is to solve this problem.

5 It is _ _ _ _ _ _ le to walk from the royal _ _ _ _ le to the nearby Anglican _ _ _ _ _ _ _ al through the _ _ _ _ el, but it is very dark and narrow.

6 The dairy farmer _ _ _ _ _ les a tune as he drives his _ _ _ _ le along the road to the field.

7 This _ _ _ _ _ _ al has a fine reputation for its heart operations; many of their doctors _ _ _ _ _ alize in this work.

8 It is not _ _ _ _ _ _ le to swim across the English _ _ _ _ _ el in the winter as the water is too cold.

9 The _ _ _ le flew in a _ _ _ _ le over its prey before it swooped.

10 You cannot _ _ _ _ le the baby now as she is asleep in the _ _ _ _ le, but you can rock her.

11 After the _ _ _ _ _ le, the wet leaves on the tree sparkled like _ _ _ els.

12 The traffic on the motorway was _ _ _ _ elling too fast; several cars collided and the drivers were killed in the _ _ _ al accident.

13 The army _ _ _ _ _ al received a _ _ _ al for his leadership.

14 Each time you sharpen a _ _ _ _ il it _ _ _ _ _ ally disappears bit by bit.

15 The _ _ _ _ le on the bag broke and it fell on the kitchen _ _ _ le.

16 The ships lay _ _ le in the harbour until the strike was _ _ _ _ led.

17 The _ _ _ el on the old _ _ _ al tin of treacle was the _ _ _ _ _ _ al one.

18 The _ _ _ le trees in Vermont make quite a _ _ _ _ _ _ _ le in the autumn when their leaves change colour from their _ _ _ al green to bright orange or red.

PROOFREADING

Read the paragraph below. Many of the sentences can be joined together by adding conjunctions. Some suggestions have been listed above the paragraph. Add the conjunctions which you think work best and copy the paragraph into your exercise book.

and   but   so   as

when   until   because

The Witboard family built the village of Westshire. They built a special cottage in the main road for Lord Witboard's daughter. She had just turned eighteen. She wanted to have her own cottage. Her cottage was number 13. It was built to her style. She loved fantasy. All around there were different creatures built from her favourite stories. It was the nicest cottage in the whole village. She lived in it for two years. She had fun. She was the sunshine of the whole village. One day she disappeared with no trace at all. Lord Witboard and his wife were very upset. They closed down the cottage. They boarded up the windows and doors. They let the front garden grow. No one could see the cottage when passing.

by Jessica Gray, age 15

MISLEADING INFORMATION

The sentences below do not make sense as they are written. Correct them and write the corrected sentences on the lines provided.

1 I am a two weeks old grandfather.

_____

2 The buses have decided to lay on emergency trips for the elderly before they go out of service.

_____

_____

3 Lewis Carroll is only a pen name, he was born Professor Dodgson.

_____

_____

4 Medieval cathedrals were supported by flying buttocks.

_____

5 Lawyers give poor free legal advice.

_____

6 A blue boy's pyjamas.

_____

7 He's a wealthy typhoon.

_____

8 Wanted – man to take care of cow that does not smoke or drink.

_____

9 For sale: antique desk suitable for lady with thick legs and large drawers.

_____

_____

10 Sale bargains – bed slashed!

_____

_____

MULTIPLE CHOICE SUFFIXING ◀ 13a

Write the correct spelling of the missing word on the line provided.
Copy the completed sentences onto the lines provided.

1 All the students in my French class are _____   **beginners**
begeners.
biginers

_____

2 Did you include a _____   **referrance**
reference with your application?
refrense

_____

3 The incident _____   **occured**   when he _____   **forgot**
ocurred   **forgotten**
occurred   **forgeted**

to look both ways before crossing the street.

_____

_____

4 I thought it would be _____   **preferable**
preferrable for you to arrive for
prfrable

dinner at half past eight, but he _____   **prefered**
prfred you to arrive
preferred

at eight o'clock.

_____

_____

5 This is a _____   **marvellous**
marvlus party.
marvelous

_____

6 Are you _____
forgoting
forgeting the _____
forgetting

Rebelyon
Rebellion of 1745?
Rebelion

_____

7 It is _____
regretted
regreted that the local television _____
rgretid

transmiter
transmitter
transmittor

will not be working this morning.

_____

_____

8 She _____
omited
omitid a letter in the sign she was _____
omitted

stencilling
stnseling
stenciling

on the wall of the restaurant.

_____

_____

9 _____
Admitense
Admittance to the theatre is _____
Admitance

forbidden
forbdn after the
forbiden

show has started.

_____

_____

10 The _____
travelor
traveller on the train saw the _____
traveler

signuls
signalls on
signals

the railway tracks _____
controling
controlling the trains.
contrling

_____

_____

Turn the sentences below into the passive. Write the new sentences on the lines provided.

1 The vandals delayed the train.

_____

2 Someone has locked the door, and we can't open it.

_____

_____

3 Your teacher expects you to be interested in your team.

_____

_____

4 You must account for every penny.

_____

5 They cancelled my driving test because the roads were icy.

_____

Turn these sentences into the active. Write the new sentences on the lines provided.

6 A friend of hers has been asked to join us.

_____

7 I would like to be read to.

_____

8 Has that chair been mended yet?

_____

9 The light was left on all night.

_____

10 The television is being delivered on Thursday.

_____

Change the sentences below: **a** from active to passive; **b** make them negative; **c** make them more specific by adding a qualifying phrase; **d** change them into questions; and **e** answer the questions. Below is an example of how this can be done:

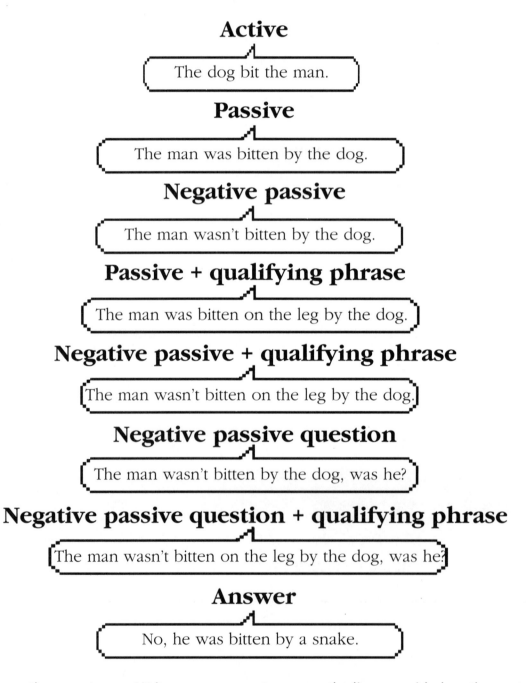

Active

The dog bit the man.

Passive

The man was bitten by the dog.

Negative passive

The man wasn't bitten by the dog.

Passive + qualifying phrase

The man was bitten on the leg by the dog.

Negative passive + qualifying phrase

The man wasn't bitten on the leg by the dog.

Negative passive question

The man wasn't bitten by the dog, was he?

Negative passive question + qualifying phrase

The man wasn't bitten on the leg by the dog, was he?

Answer

No, he was bitten by a snake.

Now change these sentences. Write your new sentences on the lines provided on the next page.

1 The man built the house.

2 George broke the best cup.

3 The nurse killed the patient.

4 The actress played the part of Macbeth.

Answer sheet

Active

1 _____

2 _____

3 _____

4 _____

Passive

1 _____

2 _____

3 _____

4 _____

Negative passive

1 _____

2 _____

3 _____

4 _____

Passive + qualifying phrase

1 _____

2 _____

3 _____

4 _____

PASSIVE TRANSFORMATIONS

Negative passive + qualifying phrase

1 _____

2 _____

3 _____

4 _____

Negative passive question

1 _____

2 _____

3 _____

4 _____

Negative passive question + qualifying phrase

1 _____

2 _____

3 _____

4 _____

Answer

1 _____

2 _____

3 _____

4 _____

Look at the sentences below. The first is a dialogue question; the second says the same thing, but it is written in reported speech.

Dialogue question

"Can you tell me where I can find the station?"

Reported speech

He asked me if I could tell him where he could find the station.

Change this **dialogue question** into **reported speech**:

"Can you count backwards?"

_____

_____

Change this **reported speech** into a **dialogue question**:

She asked if I had to lie around all day.

_____

_____

The four **dialogue questions** below are jumbled. They can be matched to make two pairs of questions and written as one sentence each in reported speech. First match the pairs, then write each pair of **dialogue questions** as one sentence in **reported speech** on the lines below.

1 "How far is it to the hospital?"

2 "Can she tell the time?"

3 "How old is Sarah?"

4 "Can I walk, or shall I take a bus?"

1 _____

_____

2 _____

_____

Now turn the sentences below from **reported speech** into two **dialogue questions** for each sentence. Write the questions on the lines provided.

1 He asked me if we should meet again tomorrow and if I would remember which cafe it was.

2 I asked her if we must be there by seven or could we come a bit later.

1a _____   **2a** _____

1b _____   **2b** _____

our

All the words in this track contain **'our'**, but not all are real words. First find the real words and cross out the nonsense words. Then you will find that the **'our'** has different sounds. Use a coloured pen or highlighter for each sound and mark each word according to its sound.

```
• Colour code •

◆  'our' says /er/ =

◆  'our' says /our/ =

◆  'our' says /or/ =
```

court   honour   minour   hour   colour   bittour   journal   rumour   your
shouer   favour   journey   neighbour   journalist   course   behaviour
tresour   harbour   labour   dour   murdour   rumour   laftour
honourable   spourt

gh

Sometimes **'gh'** says /f/, and sometimes it is silent. Choose a coloured pen or highlighter and mark the words where **'gh'** says /f/. When you have finished this, choose another pen or highlighter of a different colour and track for the words where **'gh'** is silent.

brought   slaughter   cough   laughter   night   sought
taught   dough   light   enough   plough   daughter   right
bright   distraught   draught   tough   thorough   ought
naughty   tight   might   rough   through   fought   sight
knight   thought   laugh   caught   fight   bought

'ch' TRACKING

All the words in this tracking have the letters **'ch'** in them. **'ch'** makes three sounds: /ch/, /k/, and /sh/. Decide which **'ch'** sound is used in each word. First set up a colour code for each sound in the 'code centre' below using three coloured pens or highlighters. Then, tracking from left to right, find the words in which **'ch'** says /ch/ and highlight them with the pen you have chosen for that sound. Go back to the beginning and highlight the words in which **'ch'** says /sh/. Finally, go back and find the words in which **'ch'** says /k/; highlight them in their colour.

```
• Colour code •

◆ 'ch' says /ch/ =

◆ 'ch' says /k/ =

◆ 'ch' says /sh/ =
```

lurch chef crunch christening parched chemical purchase chauffeur
chrome French technology children choir charade chronic champagne chill
stomach brochure discharge technical which character orchid machinery
luncheon chronological search chaos chivalrous chord chemistry chestnut
scholar parachute enchanting architect chateau orchestra speech schedule
psychology chance chemist machine orchard

Do you know what all these words mean? Try the puzzle on the next page and find out. When you have finished, find out if your tracking is correct.

'ch' DEFINITIONS PUZZLE

Find the words in the tracking to match the definitions and write them in.

1   A large band of musicians.
2   Total disorder; much confusion.
3   The traits and qualities of a person.
4   A beautiful flower of unusual shape.

5   The study of substances.
6   A designer of buildings.
7   A shiny, grey colour; chromium.
8   The study of behaviour.

9   Where you go to buy medicines.
10 Lasting a long time; recurring, usually illness.

11 A serious student.
12 Substances used or produced in chemistry.
13 Food goes here after swallowing.
14 A group of musical notes heard together.
15 Belonging to a particular art, science or skill.
16 A group of singers.
17 Baptizing or giving a name to.
18 Sorted in order by time or date.

19 Knowledge and skills used by society.
20 Equipment used in production.
21 A bubbly wine from France.
22 A fixed timetable or plan.
23 Kind; courteous.

24 A French castle or country house.
25 A booklet; a pamphlet.

26 A person employed to drive a car.
27 A mechanically-operated device.
28 A game of acting and guessing words.
29 A cook for a restaurant.
30 An aid for sky-diving to break the fall.
31 A formal talk; sounds with meaning.
32 A reddish-brown nut.
33 To look for; examine.
34 To chew something hard; crush.
35 Very dry, as in a dry throat.
36 More than one small, young person.
37 A formal, mid-day meal.
38 Charming; putting a spell on.

39 A question word; shows a specific thing.
40 To buy something; something bought.
41 Cold; a feverish cold.
42 Stagger; roll or pitch suddenly to one side.

43 Release; let go.
44 A garden of fruit trees.
45 An opportunity; a risk.
46 The language spoken in France.

Read the sentence in bold. The 'ch' in words 1–19 says /k/, in words 20–30 says /sh/, words 31–46 says /ch/. Check your tracking.

Cross out the incorrect spellings and write the correct spelling of each word on the line provided. Copy the complete sentence onto the line(s) below.

1 _____

Romantic	musique	unick
Romantique _____	musick has a_____	unic
Romantick	music	unique

_____
magickal
magical quality.
magikal

_____

_____

2 It is _____

diffikult	physics
difficult to learn _____	physicks
diffickult	physiques
	arithmetique
without a good understanding of _____	arithmetick.
	arithmetic

_____

_____

3 The _____

athletic
athletique young man polished his
athletick

_____ technick
technique for the _____ Olympiques
technic Olympicks
Olympics.

_____

_____

4 The children _____ **picked** **piqued** blackberries and had a **piced**

_____ **picnick** **picknic** while we watched the_____ **antique** **antick** **antic**

picnic

cars in the _____ **classick** **classic** car rally. **classique**

_____

_____

_____

5 With a _____ **flique** **flic** of the switch she turned on the _____ **electric** **electrique** oven. **flick** **electrick**

_____

_____

/f/ FILL 'EM UPS

Read the paragraph below and fill in the blank spaces with the correct spelling for the /f/ sound: 'f', 'gh' or 'ph'.

Yesterday my ne____ew, ____ilip, brought back a ____ascinating pam____let ____ull of ____otogra____s and geogra____ic maps of ancient lands. He had gone to the ____armacy to buy some medecine for his cou____. While he was out, he had stopped at the travel agency next door and found the in____ormation. There were ____otos of arti__acts which looked like statues of ancient Egyptian ____aroahs and Hebrew pro____ets and enou____ rou____ maps of the geogra____y of the land to help the traveller ___ind his way. Also included in the literature was a ___otocopy of an ancient al___abet written in a s___ere around a paragra___ em___asizing the importance of ele___ants in this society and explaining their trium____al ceremonies, including an epita___ to their ruler. Suddenly ____ilip heard a noise; he thought there was a ____antom in the ___lat, but it was only the tele___one ringing. It was the travel agent ___oning to tell ___ilip that he had ____orgotten his cou___ medicine and le____t it behind. I went with ___ilip to collect it, and while we were there, we discussed the brochure and our ___uture travel plans.

/**f**/ FILL 'EM UPS

Write the completed words in the columns.

f

_____   _____

_____   _____

_____   _____

_____   _____

_____   _____

gh

_____

_____

_____

_____

_____

ph

_____   _____   _____   _____

_____   _____   _____   _____

_____   _____   _____   _____

_____   _____   _____   _____

_____   _____   _____   _____

Match the sentence beginnings with their endings below. Mark the letters of the endings on the lines provided. Use the lines next to the endings to tick them off as they are matched. Write the completed lines in your exercise book.

1   If you want me to go with you,…   _____
2   I would have come this morning…   _____
3   We should really be doing our homework…   _____
4   If I do not catch the 5.30,…   _____
5   I would like to be a nurse…   _____
6   If we want to watch the programme,…   _____
7   I could have passed my exams…   _____
8   We would have brought some lunch.…   _____
9   They could have let us in…   _____

_____   a   …if we had known about the awful school meals.
_____   b   …I will be on the 6.30.
_____   c   …I could meet you here.
_____   d   …if they'd had a key.
_____   e   …we should eat our dinner first.
_____   f   …if you had invited me.
_____   g   …if I had studied hard all term.
_____   h   …but I cannot stand the sight of blood.
_____   i   …if we want to go out tonight.

Cross out the incorrect spellings and write the correct spelling for each word on the line provided. Copy the complete sentence on the line provided.

1 Bob put on _____ **wate**
weight because he _____ **ate**
eight too many sweets.
wait
ait

_____

2 On Christmas Eve Santa Claus will fly through the sky in his_____ **slay**
slahe
sleigh

pulled by his _____ **raindeer**
reindeer.
reigndeer

_____

_____

3 Many of our _____ **neighbours**
naybors came to our party.
naibers

_____

4 _____ **They're**
There son has gone home as he is _____ **air**
heir to the throne.
Their
are

_____

5 I hope he will _____ **reign**
rain as _____ **sovereign**
sovrane for a long time.
rane
sovurain

_____

_____

6 The _____

babie	weyed	eight
baby _____	wayed _____	ate pounds at birth.
baibe	weighed	aite

7 The horse reared and cried _____

nae
nay when she pulled
neigh

on the _____

reigns
reins.
rains

8 Your _____

veins
vanes look blue, but they are filled with red blood.
veigns

9 The children in the _____

pleighground
playground love to watch
plaiground

the _____

frait	trains
frate _____	tranes as they pass.
freight	treins

10 The bride's head was covered by a _____

val
vale when she
veil

entered the church.

Read the paragraphs below and re-write each paragraph on the lines provided, replacing or without using the "wornout" word in **bold** type.

get

When I **get** up in the morning, I **get** out of bed, **get** washed and then I **get** dressed for school. I **get** my breakfast and I **get** my books together. Then I **get** my coat and go to **get** the bus. If I am late, I **get** a lift from my dad. When I **get** off the bus, I **get** together with my friends and we **get** some sweets at the corner shop before we **get** to school.

_____

_____

_____

_____

_____

_____

got

Alex **got** a new computer for his birthday. He **got** it from his Grandma and Grandpa. They **got** it from the big shop in the High Street which has **got** lots of computers. I **got** to play one of Alex's new games. He **got** a higher score than I did. Alex also **got** a new fishing rod, so we **got** some bait and went down to the river to fish. We **got** lots of fish, but then it started to rain and we **got** wet. I **got** a cold and Alex **got** flu.

_____

_____

_____

_____

_____

_____

'ti' AND 'ci' MARATHON

Identify the profession –'cian'

Below is a list of professions. Write on the line next to the profession what each job is. Use a dictionary, if necessary, and try to use the root word in your description. Here is an example to help you:

magician   A person who uses magic to make a rabbit come out of a hat.

musician   _____

_____

politician   _____

_____

beautician   _____

_____

optician   _____

_____

physician   _____

_____

electrician   _____

_____

mathematician   _____

_____

technician   _____

_____

Mixed matching

Below is a list of 'ti' and 'ci' words (e.g. 'patient') and a list of words related to them (e.g. 'patience' is related to 'patient'). Match each 'related word' to the one in the 'ti'/'ci' list and write it in the space provided.

Related words

ambition   artifice   circumstance   confidence   delight
efficiency   essence   grace   influence   office   part   patience
society   space   suffice   suspect   torrent

Related words

patient   _____

essential   _____

partial   _____

influential   _____

confidential   _____

circumstantial   _____

torrential   _____

social   _____

sufficient   _____

official   _____

suspicion   _____

gracious   _____

delicious   _____

artificial   _____

efficient   _____

ambitious   _____

spacious   _____

Now use each 'ti'/'ci' word with its related word in a sentence. Write them in your exercise book.

Multiple choice endings

Choose the correct spelling and write the word on the line provided. Then write the complete sentence on the line below. Some of the words may be unfamiliar to you; look them up in the dictionary.

1 She was a _____
    vishus
    vitious competitor.
    vicious

_____

2 The diamond is a _____
    pershus
    precious stone.
    preshis

_____

3 The mummies in the British Museum come from _____
    Ancient
    Anshent Egypt.
    Ankshunt

_____

_____

4 He gave me a _____
    spetial
    special present for my birthday.
    speshil

_____

5 There are many black, Asian and white children in this school which makes

a good _____
    rashel
    ratial mix.
    racial

_____

_____

6 His _____
    initial
    inishil reaction to the joke was to smile.
    iniciel

_____

The two trackings below are made up entirely of real words, but some of them are spelled correctly and some are not. Find the words which are spelled correctly and highlight them. When you have found them all, divide the real words into syllables marking the vowel (long or short) before the final syllable and the stress.

'sion' tracking

sensasion	invasion	meditasion	incision	erosion
conclusion	disrupsion	television	explosion	corrupsion
attension	confusion	recepsion	inclusion	exclusion	division
complesion	posision	revision	decision	

'ssion' tracking

omission	attracssion	expression	detenssion	passion
extenssion	permission	profession	examinassion	procession
discussion	menssion	recession	penssion	transission
admission	possession	convenssion	impression	

VERB–NOUN PUZZLE

All the words you found in the 'sion' and 'ssion' trackings are nouns. Below you will find a list of the verbs from which these nouns come. Match the verbs to the nouns by writing the noun in the box opposite the verb. A dictionary might be useful here.

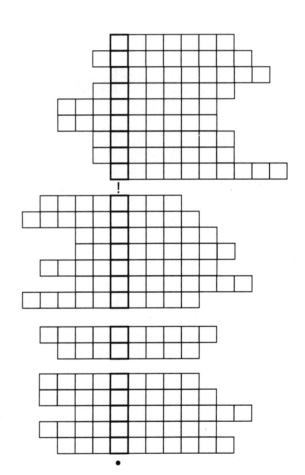

1   Erode
2   Explode
3   Confuse
4   Revise
5   Include
6   Exclude
7   Decide
8   Invade
9   Televise

10   Divide
11   Conclude
12   Incise
13   Recede
14   Proceed
15   Possess
16   Succeed

17   Permit
18   Omit

19   Admit
20   Discuss
21   Express
22   Profess
23   Impress

The column in bold says something about you. Match the words you have written in the puzzle to the ones you have highlighted in the tracking on the previous sheet.

Now use the nouns and the verbs in sentences. Write them in your exercise book.

The paragraph below was written by a very tired journalist. There were so many mistakes in the story that the editor decided not to use it. Even she was confused by the many misspellings of the /shən/ sound. She corrected a few. Can you correct the others?

The recommendasion by the politission (on the televission) added confution to the quesjun of educasion and the examinassions. The mathematition offered an expresion of divission and tendered his resignation, while the musition's interpretasion laid the foundassion for a continuation of the discusion. He called in a physisission who had in his possetion a suggesjun which drew their attension. His presentation was a plea of pastion for preparasion and revission, including correcsions before the competission. The selection for the exhibisions would be held after the complession of all secsions without omision. Information on the selecsion could be obtained from the Administrassion in their offices. The inclution of permision for a delayed decition created hesitasion. Suddenly the emission from the televition ceased. As the electrission arrived, an explotion was in mossion and the profesionals gave considerassion to delaying the conclusion of their discusion. They asked that the nassion be given an explanasion of their decition. Recepssion from the television stassion ceased to funcsion.

Did you find 46 mistakes?

Now copy the corrected paragraph into your exercise book.

Find the words in the tracking which have 'i' saying /i/ and /y/ together. Highlight the words.

experience   onion   replied   audience   beautiful   immediate

pitiful   studio   mysterious   reliable   convenient   union

previous   armies   radio   champion   dutiful   barrier   happiness

curious   readily   million   brilliant   business   appropriate   ladies

prettily   secretarial   senior   copies   business   Spaniard   furious

babies   superior   serious

Now try the Definitions puzzle below and see if you found all the words.

Definitions puzzle

Match the words in your tracking to the definitions below. When you have finished, read the sentence in bold about you.

1   Clothed in mystery; puzzling.
2   A plant bulb with a strong odour.
3   A room where an artist works.

4   Very bright; shining.
5   Full of fury; very angry.
6   Happened before.

7   The all-time winner.
8   Correct; proper; right.
9   Grave; sincere; unsmiling.
10   An obstruction; a separation.
11   Something which happens to someone.
12   Spectators; listeners.
13   Assisting with correspondence.

14   A person from Spain.
15   Being united; an association.
16   Happens without delay.

17   Questioning; prying.
18   A thousand thousands.
19   Oldest; highest in rank.
20   Easy to use; suitable.
21   Of the highest standard.
22   A wireless receiving set.

'u' says some strange sounds sometimes, e.g. 'ture' says /cher/ and 'ure' says /er/ or /yer/ (at other times it says nothing at all), and 'gue' often says /g/. In the sentences below, choose the correct spelling and write the word on the line provided. Then write the complete sentence on the line(s) below. Some of the words may be unfamiliar to you; look them up in a dictionary.

1 When I was in Paris, I took a _____ **pitcher**
        picture of the
        pikcha

        structure
_____ **striter** of the Eiffel Tower.
        strukcher

_____

_____

2 Sally is at the top of the _____ **lege**
        leeg to become a doctor in
        league

        foocha
the _____ **fuchir.**
        future

_____

_____

3 The police followed the correct _____ **precejer**
        procedure to
        proseager

        capture
_____ **capcher** the thieves who robbed the bank.
        capcha

_____

_____

4 The burglars' _____ **advenjher**   was a _____ **faler**
        afencher   **failure.**
        adventure   **failyer**

_____

_____

5 The _____
- punkter
- **puncture** in our tyre was so slow that we
- puncha

did not notice the loss of _____
- **preshair**
- **preshir** until it was flat.
- **pressure**

_____

_____

6 The professor's _____
- **failure**
- **faljyer** to _____
- **falyier**

| catalog |
| **catalogue** the |
| catilogue |

difference in _____
- kulchas
- **kulchers** was a disaster to his _____
- **cultures**

| lecher |
| **lekcher.** |
| lecture |

_____

_____

7 My _____
- coleeg
- **colleague** thinks that the
- colege

_____
- furniture
- **firnicher** of the _____
- fernjer

| fewcha |
| **foocher** will be designed by robots. |
| future |

_____

_____

8 _____
- Nacher
- **Nature** will not _____
- Naijer

| figure |
| **figyr** in the _____ |
| figer |

| priceager |
| **preseajer.** |
| procedure |

_____

9 The scholar's discovery of the _____
- prolog
- **prologue** and the _____
- prologe

| epilogue |
| **epolog** |
| epilug |

to the _____
- scrpjer
- **skripcher** _____
- scripture

| intreeged |
| **intrigued** her _____ |
| intreagued |

| coleags |
| **coleeges.** |
| colleagues |

_____

_____

Read the paragraphs below and re-write each one on the lines provided without using the "wornout" word in **bold** type.

nice

The Smith family had a **nice** holiday last summer. They went to a **nice** hotel in a **nice** resort in Spain. The hotel had two **nice** swimming pools and a **nice** beach. The rooms were very **nice** and the food was **nice** too. The children had a **nice** time at the disco. The people at the hotel were very **nice.** The family had a **nice** time during their holiday, but it was **nice** to be home again.

_____

_____

_____

_____

_____

_____

_____

and then

Judy asked her mother if she could go shopping for her **and then** she could buy herself a treat. Her mother gave her a long list **and then** she gave her some money. **And then** Judy went to the supermarket **and then** she did the shopping. **And then** she put it in the trolley **and then** she queued at the till to pay for it. **And then** she forgot to buy herself a treat. **And then** her mother gave her one when she returned with the shopping.

_____

_____

_____

_____

_____

_____

_____

30 'er', 'or' AND 'ar' DEFINITIONS PUZZLE

All the words in this puzzle end with 'ar', 'or' or 'er' and are listed here. Write the correct word in the box next to its definition.

actor   designer   inspector   processor   timer   attacker
director   master   professor   vicar   builder   dollar   mustard
reader   vinegar   calculator   driver   operator   regular   visitor
cellar   factory   particular   solicitor   voter   custard   familiar
photographer   teacher   writer

1   Someone who reads.
2   A person who teaches.
3   A person who takes photographs.
4   A person who builds buildings.
5   An authority; head.
6   A person who drives.
7   Someone who attacks.
8   A device for measuring time.
9   A person who votes.
10 A person who designs.
11 A person who writes.

12 A device for helping with maths.
13 Someone who operates a machine.
14 A person who inspects.
15 A person who acts.
16 A lawyer.
17 A teacher at a university.
18 Someone who visits.
19 Something which carries out a process like a computer.
20 A contributory part of a result.
21 A person who directs.
22 An Anglican parish priest.
23 A yellow seasoning with a sharp taste.
24 Well-known; friendly.
25 Usual; habitual.
26 An underground room.
27 A sauce of milk, eggs and sugar.
28 Specific; special.
29 In the U.S. 100 cents make this.
30 A sour-tasting sauce made from wine.

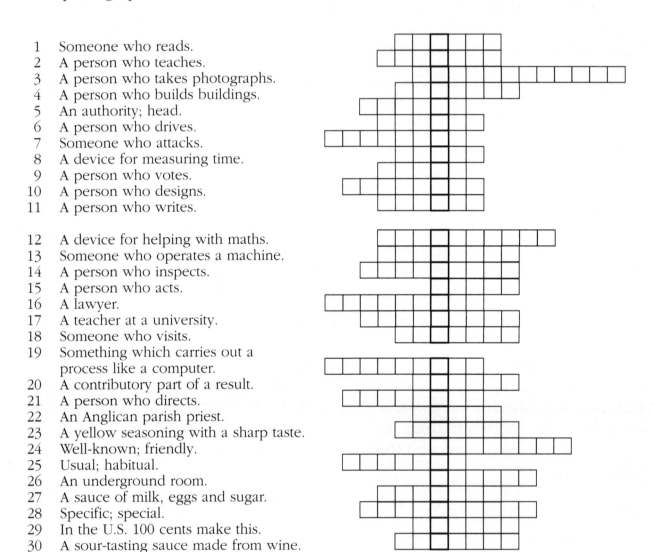

When you have all the words correctly filled in, the column in bold tells you about your work.

Use the words listed below to complete the sentences in this exercise.

anniversary dictionary gory mystery stationary brewery
discovery history necessary stationery category every January
nursery story complimentary extraordinary library ordinary Tory
crockery factory machinery satisfactory very diary glory
military secretary victory

1 _____ery Agatha Christie _____ery _____ory has a _____ory ending and we know who did it.

2 The _____ery for making cars is _____ary because the workers in the _____ory are on strike.

3 The book on the _____ary _____ory of the First World War is on the shelf in the _____ary.

4 I made an _____ary _____ery while looking in the _____ary last night – my _____ary doesn't know how to spell!

5 Margaret Thatcher was leader of the _____ory Party and Prime Minister for a very long time.

6 The beer from this _____ery is first class; it is in a _____ory all of its own.

7 On Remembrance Day we commemorate the _____ory destruction of war rather than the _____ory of _____ory.

8 Make a note in your _____ary that we will celebrate our wedding _____ary on New Year's Day, the first of _____ary.

9 The _____ary, everyday _____ery can go in the dishwasher, but not my best dishes.

10 Due to the _____ery cold weather, it was _____ary to close the _____ery and protect the plants.

11 The printer wanted to sell his own paper and was not very _____ary about the _____ery we had selected.

HOMOPHONES CROSSWORD

air	coarse	hoarse	pale	scene	there	hi
heir	course	horse	pail	seen	their	for
aisle	earn	in	passed	shore	waist	oar
isle	urn	inn	past	sure	waste	to
allowed	flour	knew	pedal	slay	warn	rain
aloud	flower	new	peddle	sleigh	worn	road
ate	gait	knit	principal	staid	way	high
eight	gate	nit	principle	stayed	weigh	fore
bare	grate	know	read	stair	wear	or
bear	great	no	reed	stare	where	too
be	groan	nay	right	stake	weather	reign
bee	grown	neigh	write	steak	whether	rode
brake	hear	one	sea	stationary	would	four
break	here	won	see	stationery	wood	ore
two	rein	rowed				

On the previous page is a crossword grid and list of all the homophones used in the crossword; below and on the next pages are clues to the crossword. Match the words to the clues and fill in the crossword.

Clues

Across

1 A time gone by; completed, finished.

4 The period of time during which a monarch rules.

6 To make aware of danger.

8 An animal used for riding and working.

11 To go from place to place selling.

14 The word used to ask for a place.

16 What you do with words in a book.

18 What you do with a pen or pencil and your hand to make words on paper.

19 A large, furry animal.

21 A preposition showing to whom.

22 A piece of meat, often beef, which is grilled or fried.

23 To shred into small pieces, as cheese.

24 More than it should be.

26 A carriage on runners which travels on ice and snow.

27 Set in one's ways.

28 What you do with wool and needles to make a sweater.

Down

2 Belonging to them.

3 A jar, often containing the ashes of the dead.

4 Travelled on a horse.

5 A preposition stating within.

6 A large group of trees.

7 Lacking colour or brightness.

9 An insect which makes honey.

10 Where your body narrows between your hips and your ribs.

12 The number after one.

13 The egg of a louse, often found in hair.

14 The atmospheric conditions.

15 The number following seven.

17 Consumed food.

19 To damage or cause to come apart.

20 The earth's atmosphere.

21 The blossom on a plant.

22 The past participle of "see".

HOMOPHONES CROSSWORD

Across

31 Correct; not the left.

33 A mineral from which metals are often taken.

35 Either.

37 Manner of walking.

38 Chief or most important.

41 To be certain of.

43 Land at the edge of the sea.

44 To make money by working.

45 Past participle of "to grow".

46 The sound a horse makes.

49 Not here, but in that place.

50 Large, important.

51 Raised far above.

52 Live, exist.

53 Route, path.

55 The person who inherits, as in property or a title.

57 Not fine in texture, rough; vulgar.

59 Perceive with the eyes.

60 To kill violently.

61 Past participle of "wear"; old, threadbare.

62 Past participle of "pass'.

65 Perceive a sound; listen.

66 Spoken to be heard, not silent.

67 The number before five.

68 Not there, but in this place.

Down

25 The number before two.

26 Writing material such as paper and envelopes.

29 A device for stopping or slowing a vehicle.

30 A step in a house.

32 A preposition which indicates the destination of something.

34 Portion of a play.

36 Opposite of yes.

39 A bucket.

40 Part of a meal, the main _____.

42 To measure on a set of scales.

45 Swinging entrance to a garden.

47 A long stick driven into the ground as a marker.

48 Look or gaze at fixedly.

53 If; either.

54 Naked; lacking cover.

56 A small country hotel with a restaurant.

58 Permitted.

59 Certain.

61 Often indicates willingness, as in I _____ like to see you.

62 A basic truth; a standard or rule of conduct.

63 A long piece of wood used to move a boat through water.

HOMOPHONES CROSSWORD

Across

70 A brief hello!

71 Strap used to control a horse.

72 Rubbish, thrown away.

73 A body of salt water smaller than an ocean.

74 Past participle of "win".

78 Standing still; not moving.

80 A moaning sound.

81 To be dressed in, have on.

83 A tall, stiff grass grown in marshes.

84 Past tense of "know".

86 What you use to make a bicycle go; move a bicycle with your feet.

87 What MPs in Parliament say to vote NO.

Down

64 Water which falls from clouds.

67 Wheat ground to a powder for making bread, etc.

69 Past participle of "stay".

70 A harsh, grating tone; husky, as in a _____ voice.

75 A small island.

76 Past participle of "row", as in rowing a boat.

77 Near or at the front; to the ____.

79 Path between seats, gangway.

82 A street.

85 Something never seen before; recent.

Some words in English look and/or sound so similar that they are often confused.

affect   effect

affect

is usually a verb:

> Her illness **affected** her work.

effect

is usually a noun:

> The **effect** was that it slowed her down.

Fill in the correct word (either **affect** or **effect**) to complete the sentences below:

1 The recession _____ed business badly in our town.

2 The _____ was that many shops had to close.

3 On television many sound _____s are used to make strange noises.

4 The shrill whistle which he blew in my ear _____ed my hearing.

Look in your dictionary and find the other meanings and uses of **affect** and **effect**. Write sentences showing the new meanings and uses in your exercise book.

bought   brought

bought

is the past tense of the verb *to buy*.

Miss Wilkins **bought** a new book on Saturday.

brought

is the past tense of the verb *to bring*

She **brought** the book to school on Monday.

Fill in the correct word (either **bought** or **brought**) to complete the sentences below:

1 My husband _____ me breakfast in bed on my birthday.

2 Then we went shopping and he _____ me a new coat.

3 Tom _____ home a cake which he had _____ at the bakery for one pound.

4 My friend _____ a game at the toy store and _____ it to my house.

Write several sentences in your exercise book using both words in each sentence.

Below are sentences containing confusable words. The confusable words are written in bold type above the sentences. Look up the words in your dictionary and write each one where it belongs to complete the sentence.

accept   except

1 We all _____ your kind invitation _____ my mother who is ill.

quite   quiet

2 It is _____ _____ in school during exam time.

diary   dairy

3 I made a note in my _____ to visit the farm _____ next week.

though   through   thorough

4 Even _____ he had already looked _____ them _____ly, Sam searched in his papers again for the missing essay.

arrange   exchange

5 Dad will for _____ you to _____ your francs for pounds at the bank.

aloud   allowed

6 You are not _____ to speak _____ during the exams.

aboard   abroad

7 We can go _____ this ship which will soon sail _____ to foreign lands.

write   right

8 You are _____ if you think that I _____ with my left hand.

Alpha to Omega Activity Pack 3

CONFUSABLE WORDS FILL 'EM UPS ◄ 34b

diversion division

9 The infantry _____ created a _____ while the tanks approached.

event   invent

10 When the telephone was _____ed, it was a great _____ in the

history of communication.

irate   irritate

11 The whining little boy _____ed the old man so much that he became

_____ and shouted at him to be quiet.

stationery stationary

12 Paul wrote on his personal _____ to his insurance company to say that

his car was _____ when the accident happened.

discussing disgusting

13 While the class was _____ digestion in Biology, one of the students

made a _____ noise.

conversation   conservation

14 During our _____ with the ecologist, we soon found ourselves

discussing the _____ of the rain forests.

immerse   immense

15 If we _____ this _____ block of ice in water, it will begin to melt.

CONFUSABLE WORDS FILL 'EM UPS

opposite   apposite

16 Your opinion is _____ to the discussion, but it is _____ to that of

most of us.

humorous   numerous

17 He made _____ amusing comments in his _____ speech.

consequence   conscience

18 As a _____ of all the lies he told, he had a guilty _____.

discuss   decease

19 After the funeral we will _____ the will of the _____d.

adapt   adopt

20 If you insist that we _____ the new practices, we will try our best to

_____ to them.

extant   extinct

21 Although the Californian Condor was thought to be_____, it is

_____ and still flying.

exacerbate   exasperate

22 Some people find exams _____ing; distractions in the exam hall

_____ the situation.

Some of these words have other meanings; write sentences in your exercise book using them.

Track from left to right to find the silent letter in each word. Highlight the silent letter(s). Be sure to read each word aloud.

science   condemn   knight   colleague   brought   doubt   Europe
whistle   knuckle   Wednesday   knot   indict   whisper   mortgage
height   epilogue   column   answer   whole   bought   listen   knife
Whitsun   knock   dialogue   align   lamb   yolk   whether   gauge   sign
league   when   scene   gnash   what   isle

Now do the crossword puzzle below. All the words in the tracking are used in the puzzle. The clues are on the opposite page.

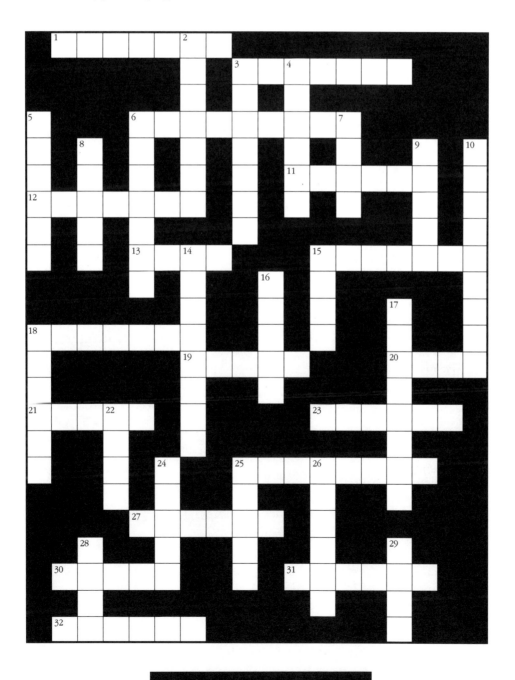

CROSSWORD

Across

1 Biology, chemistry, physics.

3 To speak quietly.

6 The middle day of the week.

11 An upright pillar.

12 The 7th Sunday after Easter

13 A baby sheep.

15 A joint in the finger, especially

at the base of each finger.

18 Bring (in the past tense).

19 Measure, judge.

20 Poetic word for island.

21 Grind teeth together.

23 Continent including Great Britain.

25 Conversation, discussion.

27 A group of clubs or teams

which compete against each other.

30 Entire, complete.

31 Distance to the top.

32 A royal honour, taking

the title of Sir or Lady.

Down

2 Pass judgement against.

3 Question of doubt or choice.

4 Charge with a crime.

5 Reply to a question.

6 A shrill outward breath.

7 The yellow centre of an egg.

8 A sharp blade with a handle.

9 Bump or hit with force.

10 A fellow worker.

14 A loan to buy property.

15 A tied fastening for a rope.

16 Place in a line.

17 A speech to close a play.

18 Buy (in the past tense).

22 A board, placard.

24 Stage setting.

25 Uncertainty, concern.

26 Concentrate on hearing.

28 Question word of time.

29 Question word to show exact

identity.

Adding a suffix to a word with a silent letter will sometimes give the silent letter a sound. This can be a clue to its spelling.

column has a silent 'n'.   **columnist** says the 'n'.

John is a **columnist;** he writes a **column** for *The Times.*

Write your own sentence using **column** and **columnist** in your exercise book; if necessary, look them up in the dictionary first.

muscle has a silent 'c'.   **muscular** says the 'c'.

The weightlifter is very **muscular;** he uses his **muscles** to lift the weights.

Write your own sentence using **muscle** and **muscular;** if necessary, look them up in the dictionary first.

hymn has a silent 'n'.   **hymnal** says the 'n'.

The vicar said, "Please turn to **hymn** number 234 in your **hymnal**."

Write your own sentence using **hymn** and **hymnal;** if necessary, look them up in the dictionary first.

autumn has a silent 'n'   **autumnal** says the 'n'

It is now **autumn;** it feels quite **autumnal.**

Write your own sentence using **autumn** and **autumnal;** if necessary look them up in the dictionary first.

SILENT LETTER CLUES

sign has a silent 'g'   **signal** and **signature** say the 'g'

Give me a **sign**; put your **signature** on the note as a **signal.**

All the words below contain the 'root' word **sign**; some say the **'g'** and some don't.

sign

signal	signify	assignment	designing
signatory	significant	design	resign
signature	signing	designate	resignation
signet	assign	designation	resigned
signed	assignation	designer	resigning

Sort the words into lists: a list of words saying **'g'** and a list of words containing a silent **'g'**.

/g/   ## silent 'g'

_____   _____

_____   _____

_____   _____

_____   _____

_____   _____

_____   _____

_____   _____

_____   _____

_____   _____

Make up sentences using **'sign'** or any of the other words above containing a silent **'g'** and one of the words containing **/g/.** Write them in your exercise book.

Map of the European Community

All the countries listed below are members of the European Community. Match the countries to the capitals, also listed below. Each capital city has a bold capital letter on the left. Place the capital letter on the line next to the country.

List of countries

1 France   ____
2 United Kingdom   ____
3 Denmark   ____
4 Germany   ____
5 Italy   ____
6 Netherlands   ____
7 Greece   ____
8 Belgium   ____
9 Luxembourg   ____
10 Ireland   ____
11 Portugal   ____
12 Spain   ____

List of capitals

G Athens
G Berlin
B Brussels
D Copenhagen
I Dublin
P Lisbon
U London
L Luxembourg
S Madrid
F Paris
I Rome
N The Hague

Read the mnemonic you have made with your answers. This is a catchy phrase to help you remember which countries belong to the European Community.

Now finish the map on the next page. The number of each country has been filled in for you on the map. All of the capitals have been marked with a dot. Write in the names of the countries and capitals.

On your map colour the countries in the European Community blue. Colour the other European countries red.

The Countries and Capitals Pelmanism Game could be played here, available from the Hornsby Resource Centre.

MAPWORK

Map of the European Community

Map of the British Isles

1 Which countries belong to the United Kingdom?

_____   _____

_____   _____

Locate each country on the map, write in its name, and colour each country with a different colour.

2 Which city is the capital of each of these countries?

_____   _____

_____   _____

Locate each of these cities on the map.

3 Which city is the capital of the whole of the United Kingdom?

_____

Locate it on the map and put a star over the dot.

4 Which body of water separates Northern Ireland from England?

_____

5 Which river flows through both Wales and England?

_____

MAPWORK

Map of the British Isles

North Sea

United Kingdom

GRAMPIAN MOUNTAINS

SOUTHERN UPLANDS

PENNINES

LAKE DISTRICT

IRELAND

IRISH SEA

DUBLIN •

R. Trent

R. Severn

R. Thames

ENGLISH CHANNEL

Map of the World

1 Which ocean divides North America from Europe?

_____

2 Which ocean divides Africa from Australia?

_____

3 Which ocean divides Asia and Australia from North and South America?

_____

4 Which ocean divides South America from Africa?

_____

Colour the oceans using different shades of blue.

5 Locate three rivers on the map: the Nile, the Mississippi and the Amazon.
Colour them red.

On the lines below, write the name of the continent where each river is located.

Nile _____

Mississippi _____

Amazon _____

6 Locate the Andes, the Rocky and the Himalaya Mountains on the map.
Colour them brown.

On the lines below, write the name of the continent where these mountains
are located.

Andes _____

Rockies _____

Himalayas _____

7 Where is the Sahara Desert? Locate it on the map and colour it yellow.

In what continent is it? _____

8 Greenland and New Zealand are not labelled on your map.
Find out where they are located and mark them in.

To which continents do they belong? _____

9 Locate Japan on your map.

To which continent does it belong? _____

10 When it is winter at the North Pole, it is summer at the South Pole, and when it is
at the North Pole, it is winter at the South Pole.

When it is summer in England, which season is it in Australia?

_____

Map of the world

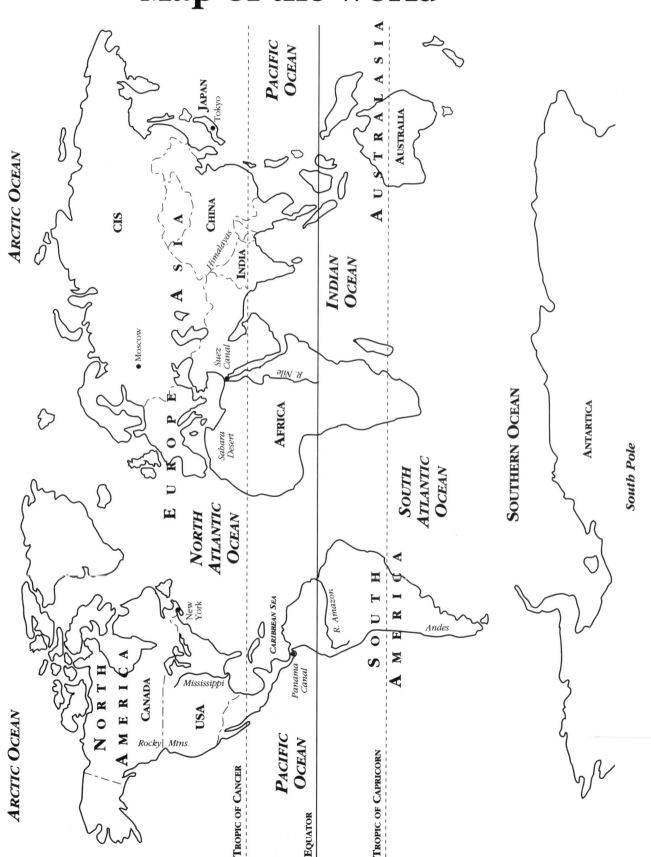

PREFIX AND SUFFIX MATCHING

Prefixes

Match the prefix to its meaning. Draw a line from the prefix to its matching definition. The first one has been done for you.

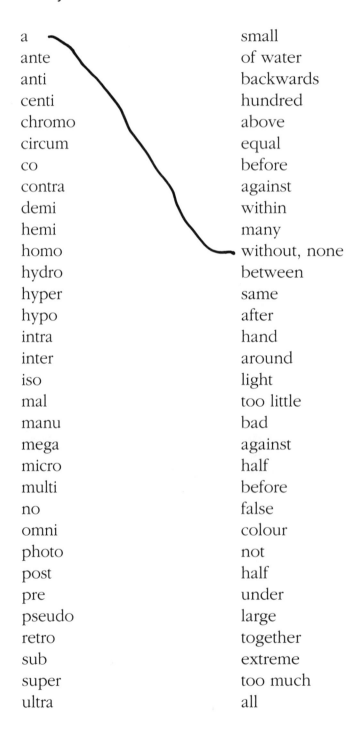

a	small
ante	of water
anti	backwards
centi	hundred
chromo	above
circum	equal
co	before
contra	against
demi	within
hemi	many
homo	without, none
hydro	between
hyper	same
hypo	after
intra	hand
inter	around
iso	light
mal	too little
manu	bad
mega	against
micro	half
multi	before
no	false
omni	colour
photo	not
post	half
pre	under
pseudo	large
retro	together
sub	extreme
super	too much
ultra	all

Suffixes

Match the suffix to its meaning. Draw a line from the suffix to its matching meaning. The first one has been done for you.

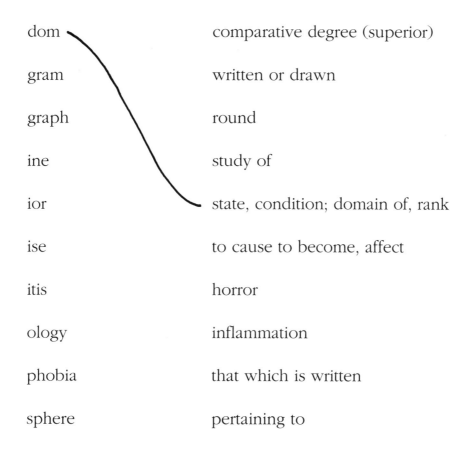

dom	comparative degree (superior)
gram	written or drawn
graph	round
ine	study of
ior	state, condition; domain of, rank
ise	to cause to become, affect
itis	horror
ology	inflammation
phobia	that which is written
sphere	pertaining to

CLASSICAL TRACKING — PREFIXES AND SUFFIXES

Choose two coloured pens or highlighters and create a colour code. Using the highlighter you have selected for prefixes, track from left to right and find the words with a classical prefix; highlight the prefix. Now do the same for the words with a classical suffix using the highlighter you have chosen.

```
•  Colour code  •

◆   Prefix  =

◆   Suffix  =
```

international   subtract   hypothermia   interior   retrospect   chronological
antenatal   claustrophobia   omnibus   manual   autograph
macroeconomics   isosceles   supersonic   hydrogen   homogeneous
ultramodern   megaton   telegram   hemisphere   multiply   heterosexual
pseudonym   maladjusted   medicine   demigod   advertise   postnatal
cooperate   microscope   pneumatic   semiquaver   appendicitis
intravenous   freedom   hyperactive   centigrade   contradictory

How many prefixes did you find? _____

How many suffixes did you find? _____

Read the words aloud. Do you know what they mean? Try the Definitions puzzle on sheet 39b.

Prefixes and suffixes

Match the definitions below to the words found in the tracking and write them in the spaces provided.

1   The lightest, most abundant gas.
2   Used to magnify objects.
3   A false name.

4   In music, half a quaver.
5   Work or act together.
6   Very low body temperature.

7   One half of a sphere.
8   To look back to the past.

9   A triangle with two equal sides.
10   To increase in number.
11   Scale for measurement of temperature.
12   In medicine, within a vein.
13   A person with godlike attributes.
14   Very, very modern.

15   One million tons.
16   One thing containing many different things.
17   Incompatible, given to argument.

18   Done by hand.
19   Involving two or more nations.

20   Of like kind, similar nature.
21   Attracted to the opposite sex.
22   Over-active.
23   An overall economic view.
24   Difficulty dealing with and in society.
25   Arranged in order of time.
26   Concerned with, filled with, air.
27   Before birth.
28   Calculate the difference between two numbers.

29   Faster than sound.
30   After birth.
31   Fear of being in a confined space.
32   Inflammation of the appendix.
33   A message sent by radio signals.
34   A remedy to make you better.
35   The inside of something.

36   To present in public for sale.
37   The state of being free.
38   A handwritten signature.

If you have completed this puzzle correctly, you can read about yourself in the sentence in the bold boxes. Now check your tracking to see if it is correct. The first thirty words have classical prefixes; the last eight words have classical suffixes.

EXAM WORDS

The words below are often used in exams such as GCSE to ask questions or to tell you what to do. Most of these words are verbs; other parts of speech have been marked. It is important to know the spelling and understand the meanings of these words. Learn how to spell these words using the look, cover, write, check spelling method; learn the meanings of these words and find them in your practice exam questions. Highlight these words during your practice exams to help you understand the questions.

analyse – describe the main ideas, show how they are connected to each other and why they are important.

assess – find the weak points and the strong points of the subject in the question.

average – (noun) the middle; in maths, the middle found by adding all the numbers together and dividing them by the amount of numbers added,
e.g. $26+15+17+6 = 64 \div 4 = 16$.

calculate – find the answer to a problem, usually in maths, using arithmetic or a calculator.

comment on – say what you think on the subject.

compare – write about similarities and differences in the subjects.

contrast – show how the subjects are different.

criticize – say what you think on the subject, giving your views for and against and backing them up with facts and theories.

define – give the meaning. Give an example, if you know one, and if you have memorized the definition, then write it down.

describe – give a picture in words; in maths, it means to draw, e.g. describe a circle.

diagram – a drawing, chart or graph.

differentiate – say clearly the differences.

discuss – describe the subject in detail and, if there are two sides to the question, give the points for and against.

distinguish – this word is usually followed by 'between'; say clearly what makes the difference between the subjects.

enumerate – list the main ideas by name and number.

essential – (adjective) most important, must be there.

evaluate – say what you think on the subject, giving the good and bad points.

evidence – (noun) facts; proof to back up your answer.

examine – write what you have to say for and against a subject, say which side you support and give reasons for your support.

explain – give the reasons for something.

express – often found in maths exams; say in a different way, e.g. express as a fraction.

illustrate – use examples to make a point clear.

interpret – give the meaning in your own words using examples, where necessary, to make the meaning clear.

justify – say why you think that the answer is what it is and give reasons for why you feel that way.

option – a choice.

outline – write about the main ideas; do not go into detail.

pictorial – (adjective) in a picture.

prove – show that the answer is true by giving the steps needed to reach it.

purpose – (noun) the reason why.

relate – show how things connect; they may be very similar or one may make another act in a certain way.

requirement – something which must be done.

review – give an overall view of the important parts of the subject and give your views backed up by facts when necessary.

state – write the main points in a brief, clear way.

suggest – often found in geography exams; using all that you have learned, say what the answer might be.

summarize – bring together the main points and write about them in a brief, clear way.

trace – write about the history of a subject starting at the beginning and following it through to the end.

Now try the Exam words definitions puzzle on sheet 40c.

EXAM WORDS DEFINITIONS PUZZLE

Match the word to the definition and write the word in the spaces provided. When you have correctly completed the puzzle, you can read about yourself in the highlighted column going down the page.

analyse assess average calculate comment on compare contrast criticize define describe diagram differentiate discuss distinguish enumerate essential evaluate evidence examine explain express illustrate interpret justify option outline pictorial prove purpose relate requirement review state suggest summarize trace

1 Give good and bad points about a subject.
2 Most important.
3 Say precise differences.
4 Say what you think.
5 Say in a different way (maths).
6 Work out answer based on knowledge (geog.)
7 Show connections.
8 Give main ideas, connections and importance.
9 Show what it means.
10 Give the meaning.
11 Thing to be done.
12 Show differences between two things.
13 Make a drawing, graph or chart.

14 Proof; facts.
15 Give weak and strong points.

16 Explain your answer.
17 The reason why.
18 A sketch in words of the main ideas.
19 Overall view.

20 Explain answer step by step.
21 Investigate pros and cons and explain.
22 A choice.
23 Differences between.

24 Tell the history.
25 In a picture.

26 Point out similarities and differences.
27 Give clear answer.
28 Pull together main points.
29 List.

30 Write in brief, clear way.
31 Write in detail.
32 Find the answer (maths).
33 Say what you think for and against.
34 The middle.
35 Use examples to make a point.
36 Write a picture in words.

The words below are frequently used in maths exams. Learn the words and their meanings. Then you should learn to spell them. Find them in your maths questions, underline them and see how they help you to understand what is being asked of you.

area – The extent or size of a surface.

average – The result given by adding a list of numbers and dividing the total by the amount of numbers added.

coefficient – A number or letter which keeps its value the same in an algebraic expression, e.g. in the expression $3x^2 + 4x + 5$, 3 is the coefficient of x^2 and 4 is the coefficient of x .

compasses – A piece of equipment used for drawing circles; it consists of two legs joined together at the top: one leg has a sharp point, while the other holds a pencil for drawing.

coordinates – An ordered set of numbers locating a point.

denominator – In a fraction, the number on the bottom below the line.

equation – A statement in maths showing that two things are equal.

faces – Sides of solids, e.g. faces of a cube.

formula – Letters and numbers arranged to state a relationship.

graph – Diagram showing the relationship between two or more variables.

hypotenuse – The longest side in a right-angled triangle; it is found opposite the right angle.

isosceles – Having two sides of equal length, e.g. an isosceles triangle is a triangle with two equal sides.

integer – Positive and negative whole numbers including 0.

intersection – The point where two lines cross.

numerator – In a fraction, the number on the top above the line.

perimeter – The boundary of an area.

product – The result or answer found by multiplying.

proportion – Related in size or amount; a ratio.

protractor – A piece of equipment for measuring and drawing angles.

quadrilateral (noun) – A geometric figure having four sides.

quotient – The result or answer found by dividing.

ratio – Related in size or amount; proportion.

represent – Stand for.

scientific notation – A convenient way of writing very large numbers, also known as standard form.

MATHS DEFINITIONS PUZZLE

simultaneous equations – Equations which must be solved at the same time to obtain an answer.

sum (verb) – Add up.

transform – Change the form of something, e.g. an equation.

vector – A way of representing something that has both size and direction, e.g. a velocity, shown by an arrow.

Now try the Maths definitions puzzle on this page. Match the word to the definition and write the word in the spaces provided. When you have correctly completed the puzzle, you can read about yourself in the highlighted column going down the page.

area   average   coefficient   compasses   coordinates   denominator equation   faces   formula   graph   hypotenuse   isosceles   integer intersection   numerator   perimeter   product   proportion   protractor quadrilateral   quotient   ratio   represent   scientific   notation simultaneous (equations)   sum   transform   vector

1   The top number in a fraction.

2   Add it up.
3   Letters and numbers stating a relationship.
4   The bottom number in a fraction.
5   A diagram showing variables.
6   Where two lines cross each other.

7   An instrument for drawing circles.
8   Answer found by dividing.
9   Sides (of a cube).
10   Add more.
11   A number or letter in an algebraic phrase.
12   A triangle with two equal sides.
13   Stand for.

14   An unplaced line going a certain way and length.
15   A point on a graph found by using numbers.
16   A statement of equals.
17   Positive and negative whole numbers.
18   The length of the outside edge of a space.
19   Related in size and amount; proportion
20   The answer from multiplication.
21   Two equations worked out at the same time.
22   A figure with four sides.
23   The size of the inside of a shape.
24   Instrument for drawing angles.
25   Related in size and amount; ratio.
26   Move without changing shape.
27   Standard form.
28   Longest side in a right-angled triangle.

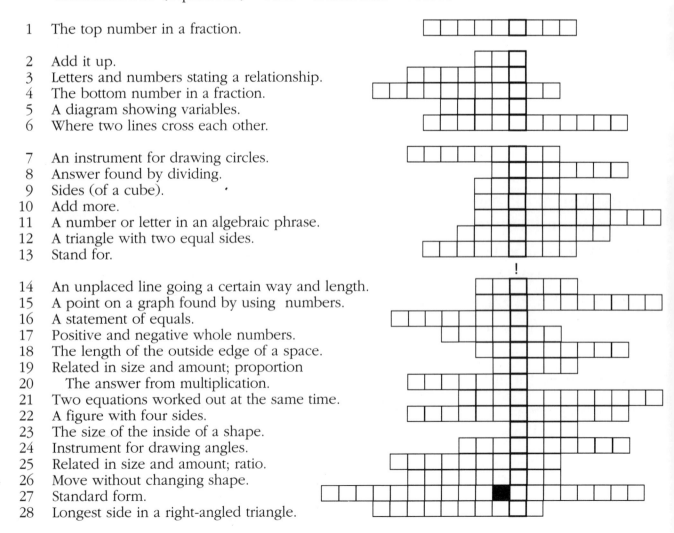

The words below are frequently used in science exams. Learn the words and their meanings. Then you should learn to spell them. Find them in your science questions, underline them and see how they help you to understand what is being asked of you.

acid – A chemical compound which has a sour taste, will change litmus to red, will neutralize bases, will react with many metals and some rocks to form salts, and produces hydrogen ions when dissolved in water.

alkali – a chemical compound which can be dissolved in water and contains hydroxide ions. Like any base, it will turn litmus blue and will neutralize acids.

atmosphere – a thick layer of gases surrounding the Earth which creates weather through its changes.

atomic number – the number of protons and the number of electrons in an atom.

bacteria – tiny, single-cell living things which may affect other natural organisms in helpful or harmful ways.

base – a chemical which can neutralize an acid.

boiling – when all of a liquid is hot enough to change into a gas.

catalyst – a substance which speeds up a chemical reaction but which itself remains unchanged and can be used again.

chromosomes – long, thin strands found in the nucleus of cells which contain information in the DNA and the genes.

compound – material made from atoms of different elements.

condensation – the process by which a vapour (gas) changes to a liquid.

constituents – parts which make up a whole.

diffusion – *of particles*: the random (unplanned) motion of particles of mainly gases and liquids; *of light*: the scattering of light rays.

digestion – the breaking down of large molecules of food into smaller molecules. The small molecules can then pass through the wall of the gut into the bloodstream.

distillation – the process by which a liquid containing a mixture of compounds, e.g. sea water, is heated to a vapour (gas), then cooled in a condensor and re-forms as purer liquid, e.g. drinking water.

electrolysis – the separation of elements in a chemical compound by electricity.

element – a substance containing one atom which cannot be broken down into other substances by chemical reactions.

SCIENCE WORDS

evaporation – the process by which some parts of a liquid have enough energy to change into a gas at temperatures below the liquid's boiling point.

experiment – a planned test which gives evidence for or against a scientific idea.

frequency – *of waves:* the number of crests of a wave which pass a point in one second, e.g. radio waves; *of oscillations:* the number of complete cycles of motion in one second.

gene – a part of the chromosome which gives instructions on particular characteristics or traits.

gravitional force – pull of the Earth on things.

hereditary – something which is inherited by the combination of the genes from the parents.

kinetic – having to do with motion.

luminous – giving off reflected or radiated light.

molecule – the combination of two or more atoms chemically joined together to form a compound.

neutralize – react an acid with a base to give a salt and water.

nutrient – the most important requirements of a diet for survival.

organism – living thing.

particle – a tiny piece, which you cannot see, of every substance which exists.

photosynthesis – the method used by plants to convert carbon dioxide and water into food and oxygen by using light from the sun.

respiration – the osmotic and chemical process by which a plant or animal absorbs oxygen and gives off the products formed by the oxidation in the tissue.

response – reaction to a specific set of circumstances (stimuli).

stimuli – a set of circumstances which create a reaction (response).

synthesis – the joining together of simple substances, e.g. elements, to create complex substances, e.g. compounds.

Now try the Science definitions puzzle on sheet 42c.

SCIENCE DEFINITIONS PUZZLE

42c

Match the word to the definition and write the word in the spaces provided. When you have correctly completed the puzzle, you can read about yourself in the highlighted column going down the page.

acid alkali atmosphere atomic number bacteria base boiling catalyst chromosome compound condensation constituents digestion diffusion distillation electrolysis element experiment evaporation frequency genes gravitational force hereditary kinetic luminous molecules neutralize nutrient organism particle photosynthesis respiration response stimuli synthesis

1 A compound which is a base and neutralizes an acid.
2 Combining of acid and base.
3 Point when hot liquid changes to gas.
4 Atoms of different elements combined.

5 Changing gas to liquid.
6 Change parts of a liquid to a gas.
7 Part of a chromosome.
8 Layer of gases surrounding the Earth.
9 A test to provide proof.
10 Necessary requirements for life.
11 Reflected or radiated light.
12 Absorbing oxygen.

13 Chemical which neutralizes an acid.
14 Pull of the Earth on things.
15 Plants' conversion of food using light.
16 Living things.
17 Atoms joined together to make compounds.

18 Parts which make up a whole.
19 A reaction to stimuli.

20 Speeds up a reaction.
21 Things which cause a response.
22 Single-cell bodies affecting organisms.
23 Separation of elements by electricity.
24 Inherited from one's parents.
25 Process of breaking down food.
26 Long, thin strands in cell.

27 Process to change one liquid to another.
28 Joining substances together.

29 Random motion of molecules.
30 Number of protons and electrons in an atom.
31 A sour-tasting chemical compound.
32 An atom which cannot be broken down.
33 Number of crests of waves in a cycle.
34 A tiny piece of a substance.
35 Having to do with motion.

Prefixes

Below are prefixes (word beginnings) often used in science. Below them is a matching exercise where you choose a prefix to complete the word.

anti: against, counteracting
bio: involving life or living things
electr(o): involving electricity or electrolysis
endo: internal, inside, within; take in
ex(o): external, outside, beyond; gives out
poly: more than one, many, much
thermo: relating to heat

Clues

_____degradable: able to be reduced or destroyed by bacteria

_____thermic: chemical reactions which give out heat

_____magnetism: magnetism produced by electricity

_____meter: an instrument used to measure heat

_____bodies: are carried around the body in the blood

_____mer: compound of large molecules created by monomers

_____scope: an instrument for looking inside the body without cutting

Suffixes

Below are suffixes (word endings) often used in science. Below them is a matching exercise where you choose a suffix to complete the word.

-ane: open-chained saturated hydrocarbon compound
-ene: unsaturated hydrocarbon containing one double bond
-ine: mixture of hydrocarbons; nitrogenous organic compound
-ate: salt of an acid which ends in -ic
-ite: salt of an acid which ends in -ous
-gen: producing or that which produces
-ide: a binary compound derived from an electro-negative element
-meter: an instrument for measuring
-osis: development or formation of something; process of change.

Formulae

-ane	$CaCO_3$	calcium carbon_____
-ene	$NaOH$	sodium hydrox_____
-ine	$CaSO_3$	calcium sulph_____
-ate	Cl	chlor_____
-ite	H	hydro_____
-gen	C_2H_4	eth _____
-ide	C_8H_{18}	oct _____

Below are a few words which are often confused in science. A definition has been given for each word and they have been used in sentences which illustrate their scientific meaning. When you have learned the meaning of each word and its spelling, try to write your own sentences using these words.

alimentary – having to do with nutrition.

elementary – basic, not difficult; to do with elements.

The **alimentary** canal is part of the human digestive system.

Breathing air is **elementary** to human life.

conduction – the process of electricity or heat passing through a substance without changing the substance.

convection – the transfer of heat by the movement of molecules because of differences in density.

Warm feet on ice will melt the ice through **conduction.**

Central heating in the house usually works by **convection.**

fission – breaking apart atoms by bombardment.

fusion – joining nuclei together.

Today we are trying to replace nuclear **fission** with processes of **fusion.**

lunar – about the moon.

solar – about the sun.

It is very rare to see a **lunar** eclipse because it is always dark at night.

Solar eclipses are more commonly seen because it becomes dark in the daytime.

meiosis – cell division during sexual reproduction in which each parent cell contains half the chromosomes.

mitosis – cell division after fertilization in which each cell contains chromosomes from both parents.

In human development **meiosis** must take place before **mitosis.**

monomer – a compound the small molecules of which can join together in a specified manner to form a polymer.

polymer – a compound of large molecules formed by joining monomers.

It takes many monomers to make the **polymer** polythene.

phototrophic – in plants, using light for food and nutrition.

phototropic – in plants, growing towards light.

Most plants which are **phototrophic** are also **phototropic.**

reflection – the unobstructed bouncing-back of waves, such as radio waves, in the same pattern.

refraction – the bouncing-back of waves, such as radio waves, obstructed, as by water, in a different pattern.

Television pictures are produced by **reflection,** but in bad weather they can be disturbed by **refraction.**

Devised by Patience Thomson (based on the Third Edition)
N. B. This sheet refers only to the Handsheet

Page	Concept	Already known	Taught	Revised	Secure
158	Syllable division: Closed Open				
162-3	'r' as a medial consonant				
163-6	'tion'				
166-70	Syllabic 'l'-'le' ending				
171-4	Exceptions to 'le' ending				
176-7	Suffixes: Multi-syllabic words				
177-8	Advanced passives				
179-80	Negative passives				
181	Advanced reported speech				
181 -2	'our' saying /er/				
183	Writing plays				
183-5	'ch' saying /k/ 'que' saying /k/ 'ch' saying /sh/				
185-6	'ic'				
187	'ph' saying /f/				
188-9	'gh' saying /f/ silent 'gh'				
190	The conditional cause and effect				
191	'ie' saying /e/				
192	Proverbs				

Page	Concept	Already known	Taught	Revised	Secure
193	'ei' saying /á/				
194-5	'ti' and 'ci' saying /sh/				
195-6	'sion'				
166-7	'ssion'				
197	'i' with a /y/ sound				
198	'ture' saying /cher/				
199	Silent 'u' words				
199-200	Final /er/ spelt 'or'				
200	Final /er/ spelt 'or'				
201-2	'ery', 'ary' and 'ory'				
203-4	Homophones				
205-6	Silent letters				
207	Countries				
208-9	Girls' names				
209-10	Boys' names Surnames				
211-3	Advanced prefixes Advanced suffixes				
216	Spelling Test - Stage 3				

ANSWERS

1 Syllable division and stress marking – 1

pắs/sage   sĕĺ/dom   sŭĺ/try   pĭĺ/low

flắn/nel   per/hắps   mŭt́/ton   shăĺ/low

fŭń/ny   as/ĭśt   bŭt́/ton   lum/ber

tĕń/nis   găĺ/lon   sŭś/pect(n.)   ăŕ/my

pĭś/tol   lĕt́/tuce   sus/pĕćt(v.)   sĭś/ter

splĕń/did   răń/som   mŭś/lin   Mĭś/ter

trŭḿ/pet   hŏŕ/rid   hŭń/dred   măś/ter

vĕĺ/vet   pŭṕ/py   clăḿ/my   lăń/tern

dis/gŭśt   mŭǵ/gy   scăń/dal   răb/bit

wĭń/dow   dŭḿ/my   sug/gĕśt   bŭt́/ter

wĭĺ/low   Mŭḿ/my   suc/cĕśs   lĕt́/ter

fŏĺ/low   ŭǵ/ly   col/lĕćt   stŏṕ/per

hŏĺ/low   hŭń/gry   vĭĺ/lage

ĭń/fant   tŭń/nel   fĕĺ/low

prĕǵ/nant   pŭṕ/pet   yĕĺ/low

ĭń/sult(n.)

in/sŭĺt(v.)

2 Syllable divison and stress marking – 2

lā́/bel   ĭ́/dol   ĕ́/vil   rī́/val   lŏ́/cal   Ā́/pril

lĭ́/bel   hḗ/ro   hā́/lo   Ḗ/gypt   tĭ́/ger

ĕ́/ven   hŏ́/ly   rŏ́/bot   Sī́/mon   vā́/cant

crŏ́/cus   Pḗ/ter   cĭ́/der   dū́/ty   bā́/by

fī́/nal   ŏ́/pen   spī́/der   clī́/max   lā́/dy

dḗ/cent   slŏ́/gan   vol/cā́/no   crā́/zy   pī́/lot

rḗ/cent   vĭ́/tal   pŏ́/em   grā́/vy   dī́/et

bā́/sin   nȳ́/lon   lā́/zy   Nā́/vy   pā́/per

Rŏ́/man   cŭ́/pid   ā́/gent   lḗ/gal   lā́/ter

pŭ́/pil   tū́/lip   rḗ/gent   pŏ́/ny   lḗ/thal

ANSWERS

3 Syllable division and stress marking – 3

lўr/ic	vĭs/it	vŏm/it	lĭv/er	Lăt/in
rĭg/id	hăb/it	frŏl/ic	măn/age	lĭv/id
lĭn/en	shrĭv/el	prŏf/it	wĭd/ow	lĕm/on
mĕn/u	măg/ic	prŏp/er	shăd/ow	prĕs/ent (n)
rŏb/in	pĕr/il	răp/id	prĭs/on	pres/ĕnt (v)
tĕn/or	răd/ish	lĭm/it	sĕv/en	trĭp/le
nĕv/er	pŭn/ish	bŏd/y	stŭd/y	trĕb/le
ĕv/er	fĭn/ish	prŏm/ise	spĭr/it	prŏd/uct
Hĕl/en	cĭv/ic	de/tĕr/mine	păr/al/lel	lĕv/el
lĭl/y	cĭv/il	de/vĕl/op	trăv/el	quĭv/er
căb/in	dĭg/it	dĕv/il	Păr/is	
crĕd/it	sŭb/urb	dăm/age	mĕth/od	

4 Syllable division and stress marking – 4

mŏd/ern	dī/al	nŏ/tice	pro/pōse
cŏn/duct (n)	ĕf/fort	nŭm/ber	pro/tĕct
con/dŭct (v)	ef/fĕct	ŏf/fer	pŏ/lice
cŏn/fīde	est/ăb/lish	Sep/tem/ber	po/līte
cŏn/fid/ence	hŭs/band	ō/ver	pre/vĕnt
cŏn/gress	col/lĕct	re/mem/ber	măt/ter
con/nĕct	ĭn/dus/try	pŭb/lic	com/plý
con/sĭst	ĭn/ter/est	pro/vĭde	sŭd/den
cŏn/tract(n.)	De/cĕm/ber	pŭb/lish	sŭf/fer
con/trăct(v.)	ĭn/tro/dūce	pū/pil	sŭp/per
dĭs/trict	dī/a/mond	prŏ/test(n.)	sŭb/ject(n.)
di/rĕct	lĕt/ter	pro/tĕst(v.)	sub/jĕct(v.)
se/lĕct	lăt/ter	prog/rĕss(v.)	
di/vĭde	lā/ter	prog/ress(n.)	
ex/cĕpt	mō/tor	prob/lem	
dĭs/tant	mō/ment	prŏ/duce(n.)	
dū/ty	nā/tive	pro/dŭce(v.)	

5 Syllable division and stress marking – 5

a_e	e_e	i_e	o_e	u_e
in/vā́dre	com/pēte	a/līve	al/cōve	a/mūse
le/mon/āde	com/plēte	a/līke	pro/pōse	as/sūme
re/lāte	ăth/lete	in/sīde	re/mōte	con/fūse
mis/tāke	ex/trēme	di/vīde	ex/plōde	căp/sule
trans/lāte	cŏń/crete	po/līte	re/vōke	sa/lūte
com/pāre	su/prēme	re/vīve	dis/pōse	con/trĭb/ute
wĕĺ/fare	de/lēte	ad/vīse	im/pōse	grat/i/tūde
dic/tāte	re/vēŕe	des/pīte	in/vōke	pro/dūce(v.)
bri/gāde	in/ter/fēŕe			prŏ́/dūce(n.)
				in/tro/duce
				re/dūce

6 'r' trackings

Digraph tracking — ar/er/ir/ur

cĭŕ/cle mejin hăŕd tupbigen mŭŕ/der widglr Feb/rŭ/ary jucken stăŕt wehen bŭŕst figot shŏŕt krundleshunec cĕŕ/tain praddle pŭŕ/chase fodgrum bĭŕth vunreds stŏŕm baddlehidrem sĕŕ/vice pumbrit chŭŕch klintinghonvre thĭŕst yekkies Sĕp/tem/ber jadlupgofrup cŏŕ/ner promet ŭŕ/gent craotrin făŕ/mer trimep sĕŕve

'rr' tracking

băŕ/row murrpebtremle squĭŕ/rel virten sŏŕ/ry doputer măŕ/ry ank ĕŕr/or mikup hickmup mĭŕ/ror tadgren to/mŏŕ/row gruplefunter hŭŕ/ry bafnich ar/rīve jibrr cor/rĕ́ct pilkumdimre cŭŕ/rent meylrejefvum ar/rānge stimple hŏŕ/ror gumpes bĕŕ/ry mirped lŏŕ/ry kefupr cŭŕ/ry plerunk quăŕ/rel streplerfrumk tĕŕ/ror mik

6b Mixed tracking

wŏŕ/ry tĕń/der fŭŕ/ther flŭŕ/ry brŏth/er cŏŕ/rect sŭb/urb Oc/tŏ/ber mĕŕr/ry wŏŕ/ry shăŕp Măŕch păŕ/rot spŏŕt mŏth/er năŕ/rowerl re/găŕd mĭŕ/ror Jăń/u/ary sŏŕ/row sŏŕt sur/rĕń/der re/tŭrn tăŕ/get stĭŕ căŕ/ry sur/prĭse făth/er bŏŕ/row De/cĕm/ber lŭm/ber ăŕ/row No/vĕḿ/ber hŏŕ/rid Thŭŕs/day tĕŕ/ror Săt/ur/day căŕ/pet

7b The royal family tree

1	Lady Elizabeth Bowes-Lyon	2	Prince Philip
3	The Queen	4	The Duke of York
5	Prince William	6	Prince Edward
7	Peter Phillips	8	Charles, Prince of Wales
9	Lady Sarah Armstrong-Jones	10	Princess Margaret
11	Princess Anne	12	Princess Eugenie
13	Viscount Linley	14	The Duke of York
15	Prince Henry	16	Princess Beatrice
17	Prince Philip	18	Zara Phillips
19	The Queen Mother	20	Prince Edward

8a 'tion' tracking

interreption **měń/tion** quorstion **ad/dǐ⁷tion** **am/bǐ⁷tion** doceration mistion **quěś/tion** contreption **aǔć/tion** **di/rěć/tion** formution **peŕ/spir/á⁷tion** protuction **cor/rěć/tion** kindversetion resiption protaction cerculetion **éx/hi/bǐ⁷tion** infermation **re/lá⁷tion** oction **ǎć/tion** exeminition reciption **mó⁷tion** prepisition **déc/or/á⁷tion** enterpertetion **com/plě⁷tion** sujestion fruitition **se/lěć/tion** **el/ěć/tion** **cóm/pe/tǐ⁷tion** decition repatition **pre/scrǐp/tion** quistion **heś/it/á⁷tion** illution politition **sen/sá⁷tion** intendtion inspiction **po/sǐ/tion** preperation **iń/for/má⁷tion** ejercation **sěć/tion** frection exhobation **fuǹć/tion** minimation **ex/aḿ/in/á⁷tion** **coń/ver/s/á⁷tion** repertation **stá⁷tion** eliction **re/cěp/tion** prepersition cansoderation **réc/om/men/dá⁷tion** eksemination **in/těŕ/pre/tá⁷tion** **foun/dá⁷tion** ginerution compersition **sub/scrǐp/tion** spation **ná⁷tion** kcrection muntion **prép/ar/á⁷tion** trition **di/gěs/tion** **sug/gěs/tion** **pro/těć/tion** serklation **de/strǔć/tion** emagernation **per/fěć/tion** condetion imformation **e/lá⁷tion** jumption **sub/trǎć/tion** estention **at/těń/tion** postion **éd/u/cá⁷tion** perscription **con/sǐd/er/á⁷tion**

8b 'tion' definitions puzzle

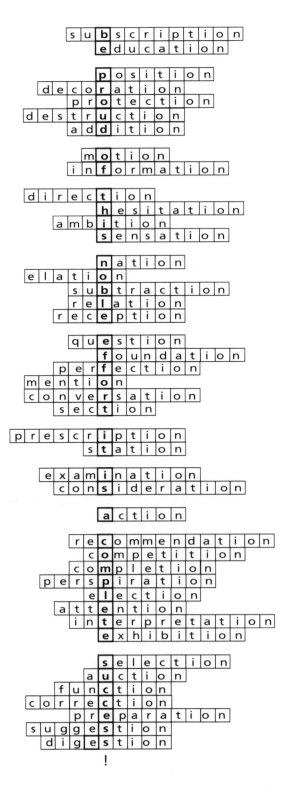

9 'tion' transformations matching

per/fĕc/tion
com/pe/tĭ/tion
de/strŭc/tion
di/rĕc/tion
con/sid/er/ā/tion
sep/ar/ā/tion
pró/po/sĭ/tion
for/mā/tion

pre/scrĭp/tion
re/cĕp/tion
in/spĕc/tion
prep/ar/ā/tion
e/lĕc/tion
in/for/mā/tion
de/vō/tion
com/po/sĭ/tion

gen/er/ā/tion
ex/clam/ā/tion
ex/am/in/ā/tion
pop/u/lā/tion
con/ver/sā/tion
ad/dĭ/tion
di/gĕs/tion
cre/ā/tion

10a Dark/l/triple tracking

'le' tracking

bugle twindle **possible** jamble **eagle** cupable tripple **rifle** **table** sirkle **angle**
idle bendle **wrinkle** truble **cradle** **whistle** rinkle **cattle** perple torrable buddle **wiggle**
simple stuble **settle** jengle **spectacle** dimble **sensible** mabble **sparkle** **circle** hurible **apple**
terble riffle **capable** sensble **uncle** mercle botle jugle **handle** kable themble **battle** jigle

Exceptions tracking

circal peepal **pencil** possibul **tunnel** perpel **metal** birdal **label** uncel **cathedral** **jewel**
sampal **hospital** cabil **original** sensibul **usual** vitel **special** obstacal **gradual**

Mixed tracking

castle miserbel **camel** **medal** **drizzle** **general** **cuddle** **channel** traval **bottle** **animal** **bubble**
trifel **sensible** appel **twiddle** sampal **maple** drissal **pupil** **fatal** **travel**

10b Dark /l/ fill 'em ups

1 A **cam**el is an **anim**al which lives in the desert.
2 After the **bug**le sounded, the **batt**le began; the soldiers fought bravely with their **rif**les.
3 The **bott**le is full of water which shimmers and **spark**les.
4 The **pup**ils in this class are very bright and **capab**le of producing very good work; they will show you how **sim**ple it is to solve this problem.
5 It is **possib**le to walk from the royal **cast**le to the nearby Anglican **cathedr**al through the **tunn**el, but it is very dark and narrow.
6 The dairy farmer **whist**les a tune as he drives his **catt**le along the road to the field.
7 This **hospit**al has a fine reputation for its heart operations; many of their doctors **speci**alize in this work.
8 It is not **possib**le to swim across the English **Chann**el in the winter as the water is too cold.
9 The **eag**le flew in a **circ**le over its prey before it swooped.
10 You cannot **cudd**le the baby now as she is asleep in the **crad**le, but you can rock her.
11 After the **drizz**le, the wet leaves on the tree sparkled like jewels.
12 The traffic on the motorway was **trav**elling too fast; several cars collided and the drivers were killed in the **fat**al accident.
13 The army **gener**al received a **med**al for his leadership.
14 Each time you sharpen a **penc**il it **gradu**ally disappears bit by bit.
15 The **hand**le on the bag broke and it fell on the kitchen **tab**le.
16 The ships lay **id**le in the harbour until the strike was **settl**ed.
17 The **lab**el on the old, **met**al tin of treacle was the **origin**al one.
18 The **map**le trees in Vermont make quite a **spectac**le in the autumn when their leaves change colour from their **usu**al green to bright orange and red.

11 Proofreading

(This is one way in which this paragraph might be improved.)

When the Witboard family built the village of Westshire, they built a special cottage in the main road for Lord Witboard's daughter. She had just turned eighteen **so** she wanted to have her own cottage. Her cottage was number 13, **and** it was built to her style. She loved fantasy **so** all around there were different creatures built from her favourite stories. It was the nicest cottage in the whole village, **and** she lived in it for two years having fun. She was the sunshine of the whole village **until** one day she disappeared with no trace at all. Lord Witboard and his wife were very upset **so** they closed down the cottage. They boarded up the windows and doors, **and** they let the front garden grow **so** no one could **see** the cottage when passing.

12 Misleading information

1 I have been a grandfather for two weeks.
2 The bus company has decided to lay on emergency bus trips for the elderly before the buses go out of service.
3 Professor Dodgson's pen name is Lewis Carroll.
4 Medieval cathedrals were supported by flying buttresses.
5 Lawyers give free legal advice to the poor.
6 A boy's blue pyjamas.
7 He's a wealthy tycoon.
8 Wanted – non-smoking, non-drinking man to take care of cow.
9 For sale: antique desk with thick legs and large drawers, suitable for lady.
10 Sale bargains – beds down in price!

13 Multiple choice suffixing

1 All the students in my French class are *beginners*.
2 Did you include a *reference* with your application?
3 The incident *occurred* when he *forgot* to look both ways before crossing the street.
4 I thought it would be *preferable* for you to arrive for dinner at half past eight, but he *preferred* you to arrive at eight o'clock.
5 This is a *marvellous* party.
6 Are you *forgetting* the *Rebellion* of 1745?
7 It is *regretted* that the local television *transmitter* will not be working this morning.
8 She *omitted* a letter in the sign she was *stencilling* on the wall of the restaurant.
9 *Admittance* to the theatre is *forbidden* after the show has started.
10 The *traveller* on the train saw the *signals* on the railway tracks *controlling* the trains.

14 Advanced active–passive roundabouts

1 The train was delayed by the vandals.
2 The door has been locked and cannot be opened.
3 You are expected by your teacher to be interested in your team.
4 Every penny must be accounted for.
5 My driving test was cancelled due to icy roads.
6 They've asked a friend of hers to join us.
7 I'd like someone to read to me.
8 Has anyone mended that chair yet?
9 Someone left the light on all night.
10 They will deliver the television on Thursday.

ANSWERS

15 Passive transformations

Active

1   The man built the house.
2   George broke the best cup.
3   The nurse killed the patient.
4   The actress played the part of Macbeth.

Passive

1   The house was built by the man.
2   The best cup was broken by George.
3   The patient was killed by the nurse.
4   The part of Macbeth was played by the actress.

Negative passive

1   The house was not built by the man.
2   The best cup was not broken by George.
3   The patient was not killed by the nurse.
4   The part of Macbeth was not played by the actress.

Passive + qualifying phrase

(NB: The qualifying phrases are suggestions only.)

1   The house was built by the man who lives in it.
2   The best cup was broken at teatime by George.
3   The patient was killed at night by the nurse.
4   The part of Macbeth was played by the actress last night.

Negative passive + qualifying phrase

1   The house was not built by the man who lives in it.
2   The best cup was not broken at teatime by George.
3   The patient was not killed at night by the nurse.
4   The part of Macbeth was not played by the actress last night.

Negative passive question

1   The house was not built by the man, was it?
2   The best cup was not broken by George, was it?
3   The patient was not killed by the nurse, was he?
4   The part of Macbeth was not played by the actress, was it?

Negative passive question + qualifying phrase

1   The house was not built by the man who lives in it, was it?
2   The best cup was not broken at teatime by George, was it?
3   The patient was not killed by the nurse at night, was he?
4   The part of Macbeth was not played by the actress last night, was it?

Answer

(NB: These are suggestions only.)

1   No, it was built by his wife.
2   No, it was broken by his baby sister.
3   No, he was killed by the doctor.
4   No, the play was cancelled.

16 Reported speech jumbled roundabouts

He asked if I could count backwards.
"Must you lie around all day?"

(NB This answer can also read: "Do you have to lie around all day?")
Questions 1 and 4 go together; questions 3 and 2 go together.

1   She asked me how far it was to the hospital and could she walk or should she take the bus.
2   He asked her how old Sarah was and if she could tell the time.
1a   "Shall we meet again tomorrow?"
1b   "Will you remember which cafe it was?"
2a   "Must we be there by seven?"
2b   "Can we come a bit later?"

17 Tricky tracking

our

Colour code
'our' says /er/ = **bold**
'our' says /our/ = *italics*
'our' says /or/ = underline

<u>court</u> **honour** minour *hour* **colour** bittour **journal**
rumour <u>your</u> shouer **favour** **journey** **neighbour**
journalist <u>course</u> **behaviour** tresour **harbour** **labour**
dour murdour **rumour** laftour **honourable** spourt

gh

brought slaughter **cough** **laughter** night sought
taught dough light **enough** plough daughter right
bright distraught **draught** **tough** thorough ought
naughty tight might **rough** through fought sight
knight thought **laugh** caught fight bought

18a 'ch' tracking

Colour code
'ch' says /ch/ = **bold**
'ch' says /k/ = *italics*
'ch' says /sh/ = underline

lurch <u>chef</u> **crunch** *christening* **parched**
chemical **purchase** <u>chauffeur</u> *chrome* **French**
technology **children** *choir* <u>charade</u> *chronic*
<u>champagne</u> **chill** *stomach* <u>brochure</u> **discharge**
technical **which** *character* *orchid* <u>machinery</u>
luncheon *chronological* **search** *chaos* <u>chivalrous</u> *chord*
chemistry **chestnut** *scholar* <u>parachute</u> **enchanting**
architect <u>chateau</u> *orchestra* **speech** <u>schedule</u>
psychology **chance** *chemist* <u>machine</u> **orchard**

ANSWERS

18b 'ch' definitions puzzle

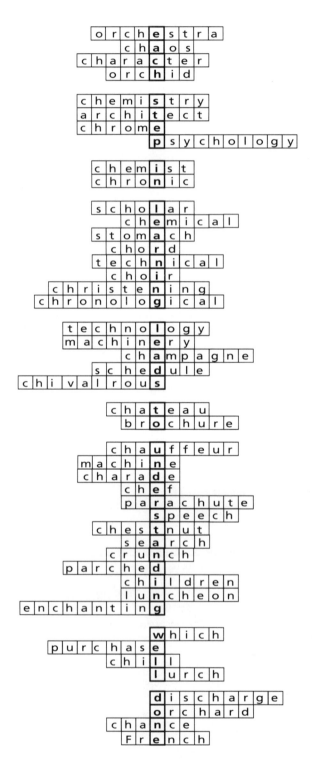

19 /k/ Multiple choice spellings

1   *Romantic music* has a *unique magical* quality.
2   It is *difficult* to learn *physics* without a good understanding of *arithmetic.*
3   The *athletic* young man polished his *technique* for the *Olympics.*
4   The children *picked* blackberries and had a *picnic* while we watched the *antique* cars in the *classic* car rally.
5   With a *flick* of the switch she turned on the *electric* oven.

20a /f/ Fill 'em ups

Yesterday my ne**ph**ew, **Ph**illip, brought back a **f**ascinating pam**ph**let **f**ull of **ph**otographs and geogra**ph**ic maps of ancient lands. He had gone to the **ph**armacy to buy some medicine for his cou**gh**. While he was out, he had stopped at the travel agency next door and found the in**f**ormation. There were **ph**otos of arti**f**acts which looked like statues of ancient Egyptian **ph**aroahs and Hebrew pro**ph**ets and enou**gh** rou**gh** maps of the geogra**ph**y of the land to help the traveller **f**ind his way. Also included in the literature was a **ph**otocopy of an ancient al**ph**abet written in a s**ph**ere around a paragra**ph** em**ph**asizing the importance of ele**ph**ants in this society and explaining their trium**ph**al ceremonies, including an epita**ph** to their ruler. Suddenly **Ph**illip heard a noise; he thought there was a **ph**antom in the **f**lat, but it was only the tele**ph**one ringing. It was the travel agent **ph**oning to tell **Ph**illip that he had forgotten his cou**gh** medicine and left it behind. I went with **Ph**illip to collect it, and while we were there, we discussed the brochure and our **f**uture travel plans.

21 Conditional and cause and effect matching

1   If you want me to go with you,…   __c__
2   I would have come this morning…   __f__
3   We should really be doing our homework…   __i__
4   If I do not catch the 5.30,…__b__
5   I would like to be a nurse… __h__
6   If we want to watch the programme,…   __e__
7   I could have passed my exams…   __g__
8   We would have brought some lunch…   __a__
9   They could have let us in… __d__

a   … if we had known about the awful school meals.
b   … I will be on the 6.30.
c   … I could meet you there.
d   … if they'd had a key.
e   … we should eat our dinner first.
f   … if you had invited me.
g   … if I had studied hard all term.
h   … but I cannot stand the sight of blood.
i   … if we want to go out tonight.

1   If you want me to go with you, I could meet you here.
2   I would have come this morning if you had invited me.
3   We should really be doing our homework if we want to go out tonight.
4   If I do not catch the 5.30, I will be on the 6.30.
5   I would like to be a nurse but I cannot stand the sight of blood.
6   If we want to watch the programme, we should eat our dinner first.

7 I could have passed my exams if I had studied hard all term.
8 We would have brought some lunch if we had known about the awful school meals.
9 They could have let us in if they'd had a key.

22 /a/ Multiple choice spellings

1 Bob put on *weight* because he *ate* too many sweets.
2 On Christmas Eve Santa Claus will fly through the sky in his *sleigh* pulled by his *reindeer*.
3 Many of our *neighbours* came to our party.
4 *Their* son has gone home as he is *heir* to the throne.
5 I hope he will *reign* as *sovereign* for a long time.
6 The *baby weighed eight* pounds at birth.
7 The horse reared and cried *neigh* when she pulled on the *reins*.
8 Your *veins* look blue, but they are filled with red blood.
9 The children in the *playground* love to watch the *freight trains* as they pass.
10 The bride's head was covered by a *veil* when she entered the church.

23 Wornout words

(NB: These answers are only suggestions; the students' answers may be quite different.)

get

When I **wake** up in the morning, I **climb** out of bed, **wash** and then I **dress** for school. I **eat** my breakfast, and I **gather** my books together. Then I **put on** my coat and go to **catch** the bus. If I am late, I **ask** my dad **for** a lift. When I **alight from** the bus (**reach my destination**), I **meet** my friends and we **buy** sweets at the corner shop before we **go** to school.

got

Alex **was given** a new computer for his birthday. He **received** it from his Grandma and Grandpa. They **bought** it from the big shop in the High Street which **has** lots of computers. I **played** one of Alex's new games. He **scored** higher than I did. Alex also **received** a new fishing rod, so we **bought** some bait and went down to the river to fish. We **caught** lots of fish, but then it started to rain and we **were soaked**. I **caught** a cold and Alex **went down with** the flu.

24a 'ti' and 'ci' marathon

Identify the profession – 'cian'
(NB These answers are only suggestions.)

musician	*A person who plays music on a musical instrument to earn a living.*
politician	*A person actively engaged in politics.*
beautician	*A person who works in a beauty salon.*
optician	*A person who works with optical lenses and supplies glasses.*
physician	*A person who practises in physical medicine; a doctor.*
electrician	*A person who works with the technology of electrical equipment.*
mathematician	*A specialist in mathematics.*
technician	*A person who is trained in particular mechanical or industrial skills or in a particular field involving technology.*

24b 'ti' an 'ci' marathon continued

Mixed matching

	Related words
patient	patience
essential	essence
partial	part
influential	influence
confidential	confidence
circumstantial	circumstance
torrential	torrent
social	society
sufficient	suffice
official	office
suspicion	suspect
gracious	grace
delicious	delight
artificial	artifice
efficient	efficiency
ambitious	ambition
spacious	space

24c 'ti' an 'ci' marathon

Multiple choice endings

1   She was a *vicious* competitor.
2   The diamond is a *precious* stone.
3   The mummies in the British Museum come from *Ancient* Egypt.
4   He gave me a *special* present for my birthday.
5   There are many black, Asian and white children in this school which makes a good *racial* mix.
6   His *initial* reaction to the joke was to smile.

25a Tricky Tracking – 'sion' and 'ssion'

'sion' tracking

sensasion   **in/vā́/sion**   meditasion   **in/cĭ́/sion**   e/rṓ/sion   con/clū́/sion   disrupsion
tĕ́/levĭ/sion   **ex/plṓ/sion**   corrupsion   attension   **con/fū́/sion**   recepsion   **in/clū́/sion**
ex/clū́/sion   **di/vĭ́/sion**   complesion   posision   **re/vĭ́/sion**   **de/cĭ́/sion**

'ssion' tracking

o/mĭs/sion   attracssion   **ex/prĕś/sion**   detenssion   **păś/sion**   extenssion   **per/mĭś/sion**
pro/fĕś/sion   examinassion   **pro/cĕś/sion**   **dis/cŭś/sion**   menssion   **rec/ĕś/sion**   penssion
transission   **ad/mĭś/sion**   **pos/sĕś/sion**   convenssion   **im/prĕś/sion**

ANSWERS

25b Verb–noun puzzle

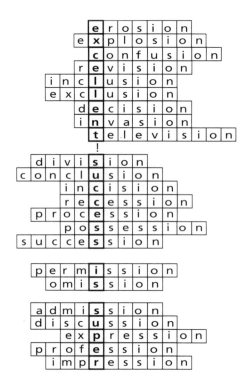

26 /shən/ proofreading

There are 46 mistakes.

The recommendation by the politician on the television added confusion to the question of education and the examinations. The mathematician offered an expression of division and tendered his resignation, while the musician's interpretation laid the foundation for a continuation of the discussion. He called in a physician who had in his possession a suggestion which drew their attention. His presentation was a plea of passion for preparation and revision, including corrections before the competition. The selection for the exhibitions would be held after the completion of all sections without omission. Information on the selection could be obtained from the Administration in their offices. The inclusion of permission for a delayed decision created hesitation. Suddenly the emission from the television ceased. As the electrician arrived, an explosion was in motion and the professionals gave consideration to delaying the conclusion of their discussion. They asked that the nation be given an explanation of their decision. Reception from the television station ceased to function.

ANSWERS

27 Tricky tracking – 'i' says /i/ and /y/ together

experience **onion** replied **audience** beautiful **immediate**
pitiful **studio** **mysterious** reliable **convenient** **union**
previous armies **radio** **champion** religion **barrier**
happiness **curious** readily **million** **brilliant** business
appropriate ladies prettily **secretarial** **senior** copies
parliament **Spaniard** **furious** babies **superior** **serious**

Definitions puzzle

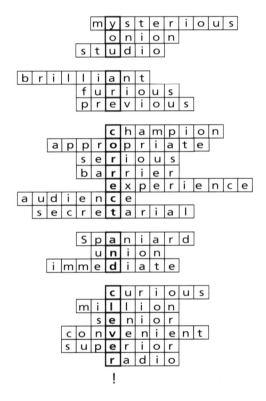

28 Multiple choice endings – 'ture', 'ure' and 'gue'

1   When I was in Paris, I took a *picture* of the *structure* of the Eiffel Tower.
2   Sally is at the top of the *league* to become a doctor in the *future*.
3   The police followed the correct *procedure* to *capture* the thieves who robbed the bank.
4   The burglars' *adventure* was a failure.
5   The *puncture* in our tyre was so slow that we did not notice the loss of *pressure* until it was flat.
6   The professor's *failure* to *catalogue* the difference in *cultures* was a disaster to his *lecture*.
7   My *colleague* thinks that the *furniture* of the *future* will be designed by robots.
8   *Nature* will not *figure* in the *procedure*.
9   The scholar's discovery of the *prologue* and the *epilogue* to the *scripture* *intrigued* her *colleagues*.

ANSWERS

29 More wornout words

(NB: These answers are only suggestions; the students' answers may be quite different.)

nice

The Smith family had a *delightful* holiday last summer. They went to a *beautiful* hotel in a *pleasant* resort in Spain. The hotel had two *lovely* swimming pools and a *beautiful, sandy* beach. The rooms were *tastefully decorated* and the food was *delicious*. The children *enjoyed* the disco. The people at the hotel were *friendly and pleasant*. The family had a *lovely* time during their holiday, but it was *good* to be home again.

and then

Judy asked her mother if she could go shopping for her. She could buy herself a treat. Her mother gave her a long list *and* some money. Judy went to the supermarket *and* did the shopping. She put it in the trolley *and* queued at the till to pay for it. She forgot to buy herself a treat, *but* her mother gave her one when she returned with the shopping.

30 'er', 'or' and 'ar' definitions puzzle

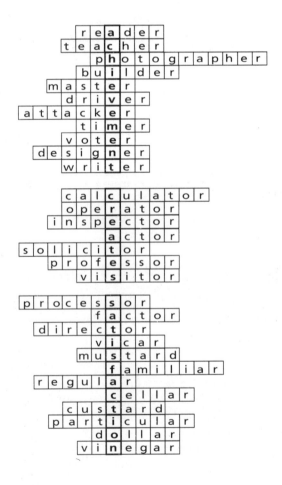

31 'ery', 'ary', 'ory' fill 'em ups

1 **Ev**ery Agatha Christie **myst**ery **st**ory has a **satisfact**ory ending and we know "who did it".
2 The **machin**ery for making cars is **station**ary because the workers in the **fact**ory are on strike.
3 The book on the **milit**ary **hist**ory of the First World War is on the shelf in the **libr**ary.
4 I made an **extraordin**ary **discov**ery while looking in the **diction**ary last night – my **secret**ary doesn't know how to spell!
5 Margaret Thatcher was leader of the **T**ory Party and Prime Minister for a very long time.
6 The beer from this **brew**ery is first class; it is in a **categ**ory all of its own.
7 On Remembrance Day we commemorate the **g**ory destruction of war rather than the **gl**ory of **vict**ory.
8 Make a note in your **di**ary that we will celebrate our wedding **annivers**ary on New Year's Day, the first of **Janu**ary.
9 The **ordin**ary, everyday **crock**ery can go in the dishwasher, but not my best dishes.
10 Due to the very cold weather, it was **necess**ary to close the **nurs**ery and protect the plants.
11 The printer wanted to sell his own paper and was not very **compliment**ary about the **station**ery we had selected.

32 Homophones crossword

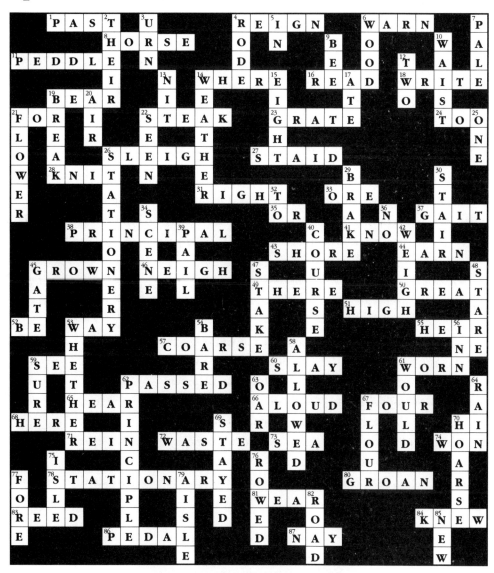

ANSWERS

33 Confusable words

affect   effect

1   The recession **affect**ed business badly in our town.
2   The **effect** was that many shops had to close.
3   On television many sound **effect**s are used to make strange noises.
4   The shrill whistle which he blew in my ear **affect**ed my hearing.

bought   brought

1   My husband **brought** me breakfast in bed on my birthday.
2   Then we went shopping and he **bought** me a new coat.
3   Tom **brought** home a cake which he had **bought** at the bakery for one pound.
4   My friend **bought** a game at the toy store and **brought** it to my house.

34 Confusable words fill 'em ups

1   We **accept** your kind invitation **except** my mother who is ill.
2   It is **quite quiet** in school during exam time.
3   I made a note in my **diary** to visit the **dairy** farm next week.
4   Even **though** he had already looked **through** them **thorough**ly, Sam searched in his papers again for the missing essay.
5   Dad will **arrange** for you to **exchange** your francs for pounds at the bank.
6   You are not **allowed** to speak **aloud** during the exams.
7   We can go **aboard** this ship which will soon sail **abroad** to foreign lands.
8   You are **right** if you think that I **write** with my left hand.
9   The infantry **division** created a **diversion** while the tanks approached.
10   When the telephone was **invent**ed, it was a great **event** in the history of communication.
11   The whining little boy **irritat**ed the old man so much that he became **irate** and shouted at him to be quiet.
12   Paul wrote on his personal **stationery** to his insurance company to say that his car was **stationary** when the accident happened.
13   While the class was **discussing** digestion in Biology, one of the students made a **disgusting** noise.
14   During our **conversation** with the ecologist, we soon found ourselves discussing the **conservation** of the rain forests.
15   If we **immerse** this **immense** block of ice in water, it will begin to melt.
16   Your opinion is **apposite** to the discussion, but it is **opposite** to that of most of us.
17   He made **numerous** amusing comments in his **humorous** speech.
18   As a **consequence** of all the lies he told, he had a guilty **conscience**.
19   After the funeral we will **discuss** the will of the **deceased.**
20   If you insist that we **adopt** the new practices, we will try our best to **adapt** to them.
21   Although the California Condor was thought to be **extinct,** it is **extant** and still flying.
22   Some people find exams **exasperating;** distractions in the exam hall **exacerbate** the situation.

ANSWERS

35 Silent letters tracking and Crossword

science condemn knight colleague brought doubt Europe whistle knuckle Wednesday knot indict whisper mortgage height epilogue column answer whole bought listen knife Whitsun knock dialogue align lamb yolk whether gauge sign league when scene gnash what isle

36b Silent letter clues

/g/	silent 'g'
signal	signed
signatory	signing
signature	assign
signet	assignment
signify	design
significant	designer
assignation	designing
designate	resign
designation	resigned
resignation	resigning

37a Mapwork
Map of the European Community

	List of countries			List of capitals
1	France	F	G	Athens
2	United Kingdom	U	G	Berlin
3	Denmark	D	B	Brussels
4	Germany	G	D	Copenhagen
5	Italy	I	I	Dublin
6	Netherlands	N	P	Lisbon
7	Greece	G	U	London
8	Belgium	B	L	Luxembourg
9	Luxembourg	L	S	Madrid
10	Ireland	I	F	Paris
11	Portugal	P	I	Rome
12	Spain	S	N	The Hague

37c Mapwork
Map of the British Isles

1. England   Scotland
   Wales   Northern Ireland
2. London   Edinburgh
   Cardiff   Belfast
3. London
4. Irish Sea
5. River Severn

37e Mapwork
Map of the world

1. (North) Atlantic Ocean
2. Indian Ocean
3. Pacific Ocean
4. (South) Atlantic Ocean
5. Africa
   North America
   South America
6. South America
   North America
   Asia
7. Africa
8. North America
   Australasia
9. Asia
10. When it is summer in England, it is winter in Australia.

ANSWERS

38a Prefix and suffix matching
Prefixes

a	=	without, none
ante	=	before
anti	=	against
centi	=	hundred
chromo	=	colour
circum	=	around
co	=	together
contra	=	against
demi	=	half
hemi	=	half
homo	=	same
hydro	=	of water
hyper	=	too much
hypo	=	too little
intra	=	within
inter	=	between
iso	=	equal
mal	=	bad
manu	=	hand
mega	=	large
micro	=	small
multi	=	many
no	=	not
omni	=	all
photo	=	light
post	=	after
pre	=	before
pseudo	=	false
retro	=	backwards
sub	=	under
super	=	above
ultra	=	extreme

38b Prefix and suffix matching
Suffixes

dom	=	state, condition; domain of, rank
gram	=	written or drawn
graph	=	that which is written
ine	=	pertaining to
ior	=	comparative degree (superior)
ise	=	to cause to become, affect
itis	=	inflammation
ology	=	study of
phobia	=	horror
sphere	=	pertaining to

ANSWERS

39a Classical tracking – prefixes and suffixes

> **Code**
> Prefix = **bold**   Suffix = *italics*

international **sub**tract **hypo**thermia inter*ior* **retro**spect **chrono**logical **ante**natal claustro*phobia* **omni**bus **manu**al auto*graph* **macro**economics **iso**sceles **super**sonic **hydro**gen **homo**geneous **ultra**modern **mega**ton tele*gram* **hemi**sphere **multi**ply **hetero**sexual **pseudo**nym **mal**adjusted medic*ine* **demi**god advert*ise* **post**natal **co**operate **micro**scope **pneu**matic **semi**quaver appendic*itis* **intra**venous free*dom* **hyper**active **centi**grade **contra**dictory

39b Classical definitions puzzle

```
        h y d r o g e n
      m i c r o s c o p e
      p s e u d o n y m

    s e m i q u a v e r
      c o o p e r a t e
    h y p o t h e r m i a

      h e m i s p h e r e
      r e t r o s p e c t

      i s o s c e l e s
        m u l t i p l y
          c e n t r i g a d e
    i n t r a v e n o u s
          d e m i g o d
      u l t r a m o d e r n

      m e g a t o n
        o m n i b u s
    c o n t r a d i c t o r y

      m a n u a l
    i n t e r n a t i o n a l

      h o m o g e n e o u s
  h e t e r o s e x u a l
      h y p e r a c t i v e
        m a c r o e c o n o m i c s
          m a l a d j u s t e d
      c h r o n o l o g i c a l
          p n e u m a t i c
      a n t e n a t a l
        s u b t r a c t

    s u p e r s o n i c
        p o s t n a t a l
        c l a u s t r o p h o b i a
    a p p e n d i c i t i s
        t e l e g r a m
  m e d i c i n e
        i n t e r i o r

    a d v e r t i s e
    f r e e d o m
        a u t o g r a p h
            !
```

ANSWERS

40c Exam words definitions puzzle

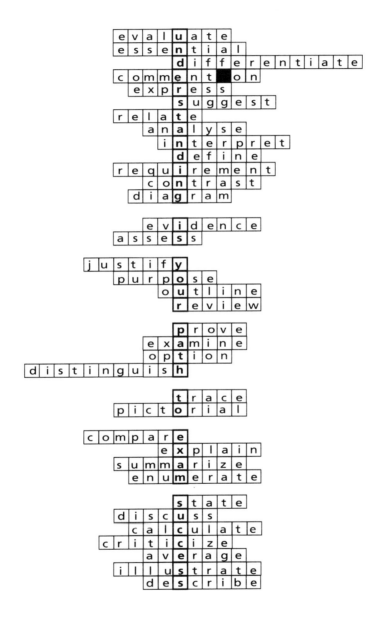

ANSWERS

41b Maths definitions puzzle

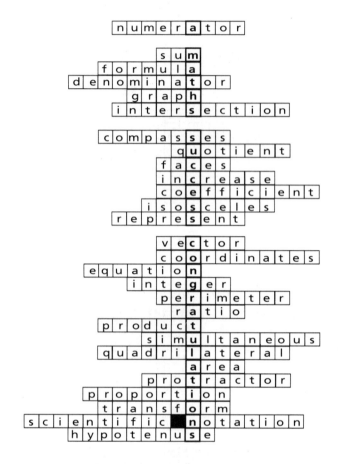

Alpha to Omega Activity Pack 3

ANSWERS

42c Science definitions puzzle

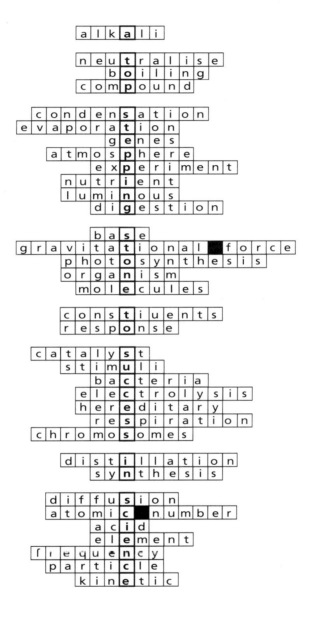

alkali
neutralise
boiling
compound
condensation
evaporation
genes
atmosphere
experiment
nutrient
luminous
digestion
base
gravitational force
photosynthesis
organism
molecules
constiuents
response
catalyst
stimuli
bacteria
electrolysis
hereditary
respiration
chromosomes
distillation
synthesis
diffusion
atomic number
acid
element
frequency
particle
kinetic

43a Science prefix and suffix matching

Prefixes

biodegradable – able to be reduced or destroyed by bacteria
exothermic – chemical reactions which give out heat
electromagnetism – magnetism produced by electricity
thermometer – an instrument used to measure heat
antibodies – are carried around the body in the blood
polymer – compound of large molecules created by monomers
endoscope – an instrument for looking inside the body without cutting

Suffixes

	formulae	
– ane	$CaCO_3$	calcium carbon**ate**
– ene	$NaOH$	sodium hydrox**ide**
– ine	$CaSO_3$	calcium sulph**ite**
– ate	Cl	chlor**ine**
– ite	H	hydro**gen**
– gen	C_2H_4	eth**ene**
– ide	C_8H_{18}	oct**ane**